Sir Gawain and the Green Knight

Sir Gawain and the Green Knight is, scholars assure us, an English poem. But to the nonspecialist it is "English" only in a technical sense. Its language and form put it beyond the reach even of readers who can make their way through Chaucer, who was a near contemporary of the anonymous Gawain poet.

John Ridland gives us a recognizably English Gawain, and a very pleasurable one at that. The language is ours. It is slightly elevated, as befits a work so finely crafted, but only enough to demand our attention. Better yet, the verse is recognizably English as well. Originally written in the same alliterative verse technique/tradition as *Beowulf, Sir Gawain and the Green Knight* was archaic in its own day; now, over six-hundred years later, alliterative verse can be as inaccessible as the pentatonic harp tunes that apparently accompanied it. Ridland gives the poem a long, loose-iambic line that sings in the lyrical passages, creeps in the spooky ones, and cavorts in the comic ones. Suddenly a poem that lay out of the main channel of English literature comes to us full sail, part of the armada that includes Marlowe, Shakespeare, Milton—even Ogden Nash.

—Richard Wakefield, author of *A Vertical Mile*

With his loving rendition of a great classic into vigorous metrical lines, John Ridland has given *Sir Gawain and the Green Knight* a fresh lease on life. I've seen several other versions of this masterpiece, but none so engagingly readable as Ridland's. His preface, too, is useful and illuminating. Here is a book to enjoy right now and to cherish forever.

—X.J. Kennedy, author of *Fits of Concision: Collected Poems of Six or Fewer Lines*

A confession: when I first sat down to read an earlier version of this manuscript, I prepared myself for what I associate with Medieval literature not by Geoffrey Chaucer—the verbal equivalent of delicate, varicolored millefleurs in charmed distorted landscapes inhabited by strange beings; magic that defies reason and logic but satisfies the desire for miracles; happy endings that have nothing to do with real human experience. And yes, all of that is here, along with the proofs—both violent and courtly—of the courage, faith, grace and nobility valued by that age. But then I found so much more than I expected, so much that surprised and delighted me by being sophisticated, worldly and intellectually challenging!

There is, for example, a detailed, fairly brutal depiction of hunting as it must have been, complete with the behavior of dogs, hunters and prey, deaths and butchering; there is the parallel depiction of an attempted seduction—a "hunt" for love—by a woman who, initially reminiscent of Potiphar's wife, turns out to be a very different creature; there is the temptation of a virtuous man, not, as in the story of Job, by Satan, but by a wise and ancient "goddess" (yes, in this Christian text!) revealed to be a relative of the tempted man, and a magician to boot; there is a token that is at once a lady's love gift, a proof of our longing for life, a badge of sin and a symbol of honor.

This is, in other words, a book that assumes, subverts and laughs slyly at the innocence we expect in Medieval lore. It upholds, instead, a realistic appraisal of the human being as he navigates the challenges of real life: surviving, behaving himself as well as he can, not doing any more injury than he can help, not claiming any more admiration from others than he deserves, or pretending to more strength—physical or moral—than he can put into practice.

The language in which the consummate poet and translator John Ridland serves up this delicious story in verse is exactly what it deserves. The descriptions are exuberant, the narrative flows and exhilarates like the wine at the courts we're asked to imagine, and the exchanges between complex characters so subtly flavored by intelligent diplomacy that it makes the dialogue of much current fiction seem, by contrast, like a six-pack on the front stoop. Read this book. I can't promise that you will find in it exactly what I have found, because I suspect that, like all enchantments, it shifts and assumes different forms to different eyes. But I do guarantee surprises, and inexhaustible delight.

—Rhina P. Espaillat

SIR GAWAIN AND THE GREEN KNIGHT

A NEW VERSE TRANSLATION IN MODERN ENGLISH

WITH AN INTRODUCTION AND NOTES BY

John Ridland

WITH A FOREWORD BY

Maryann Corbett

ABLE MUSE PRESS

Copyright ©2016 by John Ridland
First published in 2016 by

Able Muse Press

www.ablemusepress.com

Printed in the United States of America

Library of Congress Control Number: 2015955766

ISBN 978-1-927409-75-6 (paperback)
ISBN 978-1-927409-76-3 (hardcover)
ISBN 978-1-927409-77-0 (digital)

Foreword by Maryann Corbett

Illustrations on the front and back covers, and on pages 2, 20, 44 and 76 by Stephen Luke

Cover & book design by Alexander Pepple

Able Muse Press is an imprint of *Able Muse:* A Review of Poetry, Prose & Art—at
www.ablemuse.com

Able Muse Press
467 Saratoga Avenue #602
San Jose, CA 95129

ACKNOWLEDGMENTS

Selections from Parts I and III were published in *The Dark Horse: A Scottish–American Poetry Review* in 2006/2007 and 2005, respectively. Parts II and IV were published complete by Paula Deitz in *The Hudson Review,* Copyright © 2010 and 2013, respectively, and are reprinted with permission of *The Hudson Review.* Part IV was reprinted in *Poets Translate Poets,* edited by Paula Deitz (Syracuse University Press, 2013).

The entire poem was printed by Juan Pascoe at Taller Martín Pescador in Tacámbaro, Michoacán, Mexico, on a cast-iron nineteenth century handpress in an edition of two hundred copies. The wording of a good many lines in that edition has been slightly revised for the present one.

After I had translated the whole poem, I fell in with the late Mary Vezey, editor of a little magazine, *Sticks,* who scrutinized every line of the Middle English and insisted that my version cover every word of it (as several recent translations have failed to do). It is a lasting regret that she died before seeing Juan Pascoe's presentation of the work to which she had contributed so much.

Many others assisted me in reaching this final version of my translation: my old friend Russ Ferrell; the late Charles Muscatine of the University of California, Berkeley; Peg and Chris Lauer; the late Barry Spacks; Carol Pasternak; Kay Young; Carl Gutierrez-Jones; Randy Schiff; Francelia Clark; Stan Morner; Charles Martin; Tim Murphy; Richard Wakefield; and I am sure there are others, to whom I apologize for not naming. My greatest debt is to my wife Muriel whom I married while we were fellow students of Gawain under Professor Muscatine at Berkeley.

I've been in love with *Sir Gawain and the Green Knight* for fifty years, after first reading the original poem as a graduate student in English at the University of California in Berkeley. More to the point, a year later I first had the chance to teach it, largely in paraphrase, to undergraduates at Los Angeles State College—as I did again at the University of California, Santa Barbara, in the 1970s. Always I kept hoping I could find my way to transposing the whole poem into Modern English someday. That day finally came in 2003, the summer before I retired from UCSB. From 2005 until her untimely death in 2009, I became extremely indebted to the assistance of Mary Veazey, editor of *Sticks,* a quirky little magazine out of Maplesville, Alabama, as far from Los Angeles or New York as the unknown Northern Midlands court where the poem was first presented was from London. Mary's spirit of relentless accuracy has stayed with me during my final revisions.

Why does *Sir Gawain and the Green Knight* demand to be translated when his contemporary Chaucer doesn't? Today, as in 1960, I believe that very few non-graduate students dare to venture into the thickets of the poem's Northern West Midlands dialect of Middle English. Even the accessibility of Chaucer's Southern dialect suffered, thanks to the Great Vowel Shift of the Fifteenth Century, when our vowels stopped sounding like those of present-day European languages. Chaucer's versification suffered even more from the loss of the final unaccented *e* on many words, eliminating enough syllables to make his meter unscannable and almost unreadable. To correct this flaw, as he saw it, Alexander Pope, three centuries after Chaucer's time and the same number before ours, translated Chaucer into proper Modern English verse. Chaucer's London dialect proved fittest to survive the struggle to create Modern English, pushing aside the Northern Midlands speech of the unknown author of *Sir Gawain* (whose anonymity is simply another indignity). Bad luck for the Unknown Poet and his dialect, but against that, we should set his extraordinary good luck in the poem's having survived at all, since it exists in a single scribal manuscript, leather bound in a small volume with three other poems of similar length and probably, scholars agree, written by the same author. Against that, there are nearly a hundred manuscript copies of *The Canterbury Tales,* not even counting their first printed publication by William Thynne in 1532. The *Gawain* manuscript was tucked away in the private library of Sir Robert Cotton, which caught fire in the early eighteenth century, not harming this particular book, fortunately, although it was not read and edited by anyone until the early nineteenth century. It could not be widely read in Modern English until Jessie Weston's 1898 prose translation.

Despite its obscure dialect, however, *Sir Gawain and the Green Knight* so clearly belongs on the shelf of Essential Medieval English Literature that numerous translators have tried to "carry it across" (the root meaning of *trans-late*) into Modern English. I have consulted more than a dozen translations while making my own. My version differs from most others in two ways: first, I am determined to maintain the meanings of as many of the original words as possible while bringing them across from Middle English, without forcing a modern cognate word out of its common usage. This makes my lines longer than others in total word count, though the line contents and numbering are the same as the original. And second, I believe this is the only translation written in a familiar modern meter.

This is a controversial claim. Brian Stone (1959), T.H. Banks (1962), Marie Boroff (1967), Burton Raffel (1970), J.R.R. Tolkien (1975), William Vantuono (1999), Simon Armitage (2006), Bernard O'Donoghue (2007), and quite a few others, all have done battle with alliterative strong-stress verse. This meter, which was native in Old English, had been invaded and transformed, three centuries before the *Gawain* poet's time, by French accentual-syllabic measures. The extent of the conversion is evident in Chaucer's practice and in his famous put-down of the *rum-ram-ruf* alliterative verse that some of his contemporaries were writing (particularly William Langland in the popular *Piers Plowman).* Whether they were *still* writing it in the fourteenth century, or *reviving* it, seems to be a scholarly argument which I'll have to watch from the sidelines, but since Langland and the *Gawain* poet are sometimes included as part of an Alliterative Revival, these twentieth and twenty-first century translators have been striving to *revive* a *revival.* Alliterative accentual verse has not remained a major poetic tradition outside of the translation of Old or Middle English poems, except for the occasional tours de force by W.H. Auden or Richard Wilbur, and others, of whom in her foreword, Corbett mentions Anthony Hecht, Lewis Turco, Joshua Mehigan and herself.

Today's readers therefore have to be taught how to read it aloud: put extra emphasis on the stressed syllables that begin with the same sound, and some others that don't alliterate, and take a pause in the middle of the line. It's as if an American football team suddenly had to play by the rules of soccer (no hands!) or of rugby (no forward passes!). Alliterative accentual verse in Modern English is, for a modern reader, forced, pedantic, or pedagogic—none of which is fun. And the original *Gawain and the Green Knight* (a title supplied by editors, not by the manuscript) is as much fun to read as anything in Chaucer.

One solution to this difficulty is to translate the poem into prose, like Neilson and Webster in 1916, or Gordon Hall Gerould in 1929, or free verse, like W.S. Merwin in 2002, but this choice loses the momentum with which regular meter can sweep a reader of long poems along. Such readers must be at heart *listeners*. Poems were read aloud in the fourteenth century, as they were five hundred years before in the time of *Beowulf*. There's a small contemporary painting of Chaucer reading from a lectern to a "noble audience" in London, and scholars suppose the *Gawain* poet must have done the same in his provincial court. Another solution to the problem of making it go in verse, which no one else has attempted recently, is to adopt a familiar accentual-syllabic meter, such as what Frost called "loose iambics"—mostly iambic feet, with a good number of anapests. Mine is perhaps closer to "loose anapestics" with a good sprinkling of iambs, but who's counting? I didn't scan or classify my meter while writing, but Corbett in her foreword and an article online[1] found it a generally satisfying solution.

Since this sort of meter has been familiar for centuries, it doesn't need to have its rules explained. In the long-lined strophes I aim for seven accents to the line, which could therefore be heard as a one-line merger of the first two lines of the traditional ballad quatrain, where four beats are followed by three. This stanza is heard in songs from nursery rhymes on up to "Sir Patrick Spens" and beyond. With such a familiar verse form, the varied natural stress levels of speech accommodate the metrical pattern of unaccented and accented syllables, and when the lines of this translation are read as normal speech by a native speaker of English, I believe the meter will assert itself. Variations in speech stress (and pitch and juncture and all the other elements of language) contribute variety to the steady accentual beats of the meter, while the regularity of that meter imposes a higher degree of order on the speech stresses:

> Soon they gave tongue and the search was on along one side of the marsh

I would scan this line as "loose iambics," with four iambs, two anapests, and an initial trochee:

> /   x |x   / |x   x   / |x   /|x / |x   / |x   x   /
> Soon they gave tongue and the search was on along one side of the marsh,
>   *trochee*   *iamb*   *anapest*   *iamb*   *iamb*   *iamb*   *anapest*

---

1   http://www.barefootmuse.com/archives/issue9/corbett.htm

There is a barely noticeable pause after the fourth foot—a caesura but a light one, a surface scratch not a deep cut. Following the fourth beat, such a pause threatens to turn my measure back into ballad meter, and with rhymes on the end, these lines would lapse into the cumbersome "Fourteeners" (seven iambic feet without variation) of the mid-sixteenth century. That's why I kept end rhymes off the long lines, and even not rhyming I had to work hard to avoid the inevitable singsong characteristic of this form:

> Soon they gave tongue and the search was on
> Along one side of the <u>vale</u>,
> The huntsmen urging on those hounds
> That had first picked up the <u>trail</u>.

Formatted like this the rhythm would break into awkward short measures, rousing the anticipation of end rhyme every two lines: the 2530 lines of the original poem would become a ballad of about 5000 lines—an English language record, perhaps, but not an enviable one; and they would have to break into quatrains, further stultifying the movement of the whole poem. Laid out as two unrhymed lines instead of four, however, the pause seems fainter, and the line ends are not tagged as hard as they would be with rhymes:

> Soon they gave tongue and the search was on along one side of the marsh,
> The huntsmen urging on those hounds that had first picked up the trail.

The poet almost always end-stops his lines: on a very few occasions when he doesn't, you take notice. And seldom do the lines pair off into what would be quatrains in regular ballad meter. The poet is a master of long sentences.

Unlike modern translators who commit themselves to reviving the alliterative-accentual tradition, thus requiring a specified number and placement of alliterating syllables per line, I have ladled on the alliteration ad lib as an ornament—and the style of the original is as lavishly ornamented as an illuminated manuscript, as Corbett notes independently. At some point early on I realized I was dealing out alliterations in a sort of poetic poker game: three *s*'s in the first line above beat a pair of *h*'s in the second line, the latter a "weak" hand, but better than not even a pair, like quite a few of my lines, though internal rhyming may strengthen some. When I noticed this dancingly alliterative line in the third long strophe of the story (after the two-strophe historical backstory), I realized the potential of this analogy:

> A delightful din all down the day, and dancing all the night

(*Five d's!*) It was a game that helped keep me drawing from the deck of the thesaurus and the dictionary for fresh alliterations. Ad hoc or random alliteration could emulate the sound effects of the original without imitating the exact pattern, deceiving some readers into thinking I was in fact composing in accentual alliterative verse.

The original manuscript set ornamented initial letters at four places, tacitly dividing the poem into Parts that scholars have called "Fits" (a medieval term which I have not used here), and these are as artfully placed as Dickens's novels' installment endings: I'll leave the reader to test that point. Within those Parts, a pattern is set of each long stanza or strophe forming a distinct unit, which is broken only once, quite startlingly. During Part III, while the lord of the castle is out hunting animals and his wife is back home in the castle hunting Gawain, the action cuts back and forth from scene to scene with remarkably cinematic skill, as if a film script specified "EXTERIOR. DAY. FOREST SCENE.—INTERIOR. MORNING LIGHT THROUGH BEDROOM WINDOWS." Sometimes the scenes are separated among strophes, but at other times they are merged, cutting from one to the other even in mid-sentence.

At the end of each strophe comes what is called the "bob and wheel" stanza, which really *is* a stanza, in that it is always five lines long, rhyming *ababa,* and often including some alliteration, which the poet's habitual practice can't help slipping in. The first line "bob" contains a single iambic foot, the four lines of the "wheel" each have three. In doing this, the poet shows himself adept at the newer style brought over from France as well as the older Germanic meter, and shows us he can use them both in a single poem—it's a unique metrical performance as far as I know. Some critics have found these little stanzas extraneous, simply summarizing what has been, or is soon to be, told. I do not agree at all; for example in line 147, when the huge, "awe-inspiring" man rushes into the Christmas festivities at Camelot, for eleven lines his bulk and handsomeness are carefully described. The most unusual detail, however, which surely anyone would notice first, and which is keyed in the poem's title, is withheld until the very last word of the bob-and-wheel (italics mine):

> Men marveled at the hue
> That stained him with its sheen;
> Charging into their view,
> He was—face and all—*bright green!*

(These little stanzas, by the way, since I was determined to keep them rhyming, even slantingly, took sometimes as long to translate as their whole strophe.)

★ ★ ★

So, BEYOND ALL THE TWISTS AND TURNS of the story and the lustrous descriptive details, can we say what the whole poem is "about"? The original audience must have been taken by Gawain's exemplification of the virtues of a Christian courtly knight, while noticing that since he was only human, he could fall short of perfection—an encouragement to ordinary sinners. That is all very Medieval and properly so. But for modern non-Medievalists? I think it's largely about keeping cool—about *playing* it cool, even—when things heat up: keeping a cool head in order to literally *keep* your head.

Like all masterpieces, the poem makes us aware of many particulars we may not have considered before. For example, against my expectations, I found the hunting and butchering scenes quite as fascinating and as delicately described as the bedroom ones. I knew enough about the latter to imagine and appreciate them, but never having been a hunter, I had a lot to learn about the former: there are important differences between Red Deer, which are "harts" and "hinds," and Fallow Deer, which are "bucks" and "does." And "fallow" has nothing to do with an unplowed field, but derives from the Old English *fealu* for "yellow." In the end, I thought, if I were starving in the woods, I could butcher a deer by following the step-by-step instructions in the poem. These graphic details may distress modern readers with vegetarian leanings. But those hunters didn't, to quote W.S. Merwin, "maul and murder living creatures" for sport. The huge heap ("quarry") of venison is divided up for each member of the hunting party to take home his share: in that culture and climate, where nothing grows in winter, the men had to be hunters, and this was *food* to keep them and their families alive.

How the hunting scenes are played against the bedroom ones has been much debated—what human qualities each animal represents and how each chase lines up with Gawain's actions. I think the specific reality of the narrative is too dense for this to be of much immediate concern to the reader or listener. I believe we are being invited to keep our eyes on what the "camera" shows and our ears on the sounds the microphones pick up. One thing that strikes me is how well the poet knows both the man's world of hunting and the woman's world of the bedroom and hall, and how the poem lets us live equally in each. Both sets of action have moral and even spiritual implications that are not dismissible as "typically Medieval" but provide something for "typical" Modernists—or Post-Modernists—to ponder. The conflict between Gawain's natural instinct to survive and his religious and courtly principles is just as relevant in today's world of religious, moral, and patriotic confusions.

★ ★ ★

Some Technical Details

1. The syllables of the name *Gawain* (I have ignored the occasional manuscript spelling *Wawain)* are so nearly equally stressed that I have sometimes used it as a natural iamb rather than a trochee.

2. The poem's verbs are constantly switching from past tense to the historical present. Sometimes I think the shift from past to present worked like a sudden zoom to closeup in a movie, but I have been persuaded by several readers that this is too confusing in Modern English and so have stuck to the past tenses consistently.

3. To have provided the Middle English text on verso pages would require a professionally qualified specialist to resolve the scores of cruxes that the manuscript presents, as Andrews and Waldron note in their comprehensive edition of the *Poems of the Pearl Manuscript* (2002). The Internet can provide acceptable versions of the original text. My purpose has been to make a modern poem that is as true to the meanings as to the spirit of that original, and therefore to be readable without the Middle English facing it.

John Ridland
Santa Barbara, California

Having read John Ridland's translation with pleasure part by part, as the parts appeared in magazines, I am delighted to see it and read it whole at last. Like Ridland, I fell in love early with *Sir Gawain and the Green Knight*. The poem has been bowling readers over in just this way ever since its discovery in Sir Robert Cotton's collection, and its later presentation to the world in print in 1824. Technically brilliant, narratively gripping, and visually gorgeous, it has everything a reader could want, and it needs only to be made accessible in modern English.

The poem's pull on me, as on many other readers, depended not only on its story, a romance in the Arthurian tradition, but also on its intricate metrical and alliterative pattern. A small sample of the meter appears below. The poem uses a four-stress line, divided by a caesura, with at least two of the stresses and as many as four alliterating with one another. Each strophe of these lines is wrapped up with a four-line "wheel" (of a five-line "bob and wheel") in rhymed trimeter. As I've written elsewhere, in the essay that Ridland refers to in his introduction, I was a little slow to believe that modern readers have trouble with the four-stress alliterative line, or that the poem needs to be translated in something other than its original meter.

The reason it does need to be translated, for everyone who is not a specialist in Middle English, is laid out in the introduction. The question is how the poem's sounds should be handled in translation, since sound is such a huge element of the poem's artistry. Is the seven-foot line—called variously heptameter or ballad meter or fourteeners—an appropriate tool for balancing concern for the poem's sounds with care for its meaning? When I first met the idea, I needed convincing. Happily, I have been convinced by the work you see here.

The essence of the *Gawain* poet's method is extravagance. Extravagance, as Robert Frost has said in a lecture[2], is a legitimate feature of poetry, and this poem's original surface is a fireworks display of rhythmic and sonic effects. But all that dazzle can leave a translator

---

2   Frost, R. (1962). "On Extravagance: A Talk." In *Robert Frost. Collected Poems, Prose and Plays*, eds. R. Poirier and M. Richardson. New York: Library of America, 1995, pp. 739–740

cross-eyed. One difficulty is that many of the alliterating words of the poet's Northwest Midland dialect have no direct survivals in contemporary English. We can see a little of this in the sample passage below. Tulk, for example, translated "man" or "fighting man" or "soldier," has no modern equivalent that starts with t. Neither does trammes, meaning "devices" or "stratagems." To stick with the pattern of alliteration and stress, one must come up with approximations, words that may hit the right sound but only sidle up to the original meaning. All translation risks this loss, but strict form sharpens the risk.

The second difficulty is the way the modern reader expects to hear a four-stress line. The modern poets who sometimes use it (Auden, Wilbur, Hecht, Lewis Turco, and more recently Joshua Mehigan and I) tend to stick to lines of eight to ten syllables, like this one from Wilbur's "Lilacs":

These laden lilacs   at the lawn's end

To show how hard it is to fit the *Gawain* poet's lines into that space, I present the opening lines of the Middle English with their spelling modernized, their alliterating and stressed syllables marked with boldface type, and their syllables counted:

Sithen the **sege** and the as**saut** watz **sesed** at **Troye,** (15 syllables)
The borgh **britt**ened and **brent** to **brond**ez and **ask**ez, (13)
The **tulk** þat the **tram**mes of **tres**oun ther **wroght** (11)
Watz **tried** for his **trich**erie, the **trew**est on **erthe:** (15)
Hit watz **En**nias the **ath**el, and his **high**e **kynd**e, (14)
That sithen **depreced prou**inces, and **patrounes** bi**come** (16)
Welneghe of al the **wele** in the **west iles.** (13)

To boil those long lines down to modern accentual tetrameter, a translator has to decide, over and over, which words to jettison. This means even further loss of meaning.

Ridland's great insight is that heptameter is roomy and unconstricted, as well as being satisfying to the modern ear. The alliteration is not lost; the heptameter allows the alliterating words to fall naturally within the line. Most importantly, it gives the translator enough space to accommodate all the words in even the longest, most syllable-packed lines of the original.

And there are very important reasons to preserve as much of the poem's substance as possible. One reason is that we know nothing, apart from *Gawain* and the other poems in the same manuscript, about the poem's author, his background, his milieu, and his reasons for writing. Only the poems tell us about the poet. To dig deeply into the poem, we want answers to questions like these: Is this very court-centered poem connected with royal patronage? If so, was the author connected to Richard II, he of the very aristocratic, free-spending, and unwarlike ways? Does the reference to Arthur as childgered (which might be translated "childish" or "childlike" or "boyish" or "youthful") relate to the very young accession of Richard, and to criticisms of his policies? Is there some insinuation in the fact that Gawain, who comes from the royal court, fails a test of courtliness that his provincial hosts are judging? Nearly every fact of the author's life that we might care about is lost to history and unavailable as a way to illuminate the poem. So all the meaning we have, we need to hang onto.

If you've come to this very accessible rendering for pure entertainment, you might not be interested in those historical questions. But there's another important reason to give the reader all the words there are: the poet's extravagance of descriptive detail. The *Gawain* poet is, in Burton Raffel's phrase, incomparably visual, and his descriptions are pleasurable in the same way as the exquisite miniatures of the Duc de Berry's manuscript book of hours, *Les Très Riches Heures*. Panoramas of banqueting and hunting, closely observed rituals of dressing, arming, and game preparation, and rich descriptions of landscape and weather—Ridland's translation presents these in all their delightful, over-the-top particularity.

Ridland also meets the challenge of the poem's traditional formulas and repeating epithets. Modern audiences look to poets for originality and surprise, but medieval audiences valued and expected these repetitions, especially in a romance. The present translation strikes a pleasing balance between tradition and freshness.

The result is that a contemporary reader can experience the same sort of pleasures that the poet wanted to provide for the audience he had in mind. That was almost certainly a listening audience. It may have been a courtly audience of the poet's peers, or it may have been a less august company but still a company that shared the old values of courtliness, knighthood, and romance—values that were beginning to be seen as stuffy and old fashioned but that were still alive. What the poet's audience wanted was delight: delight of the ear and of the eye, and also of the seductions of a good story, in which many story lines interweave and still untangle themselves at the end—satisfyingly, but with a hint of ambiguity. This is the experience that gives the poem the pull it had on its first audiences, and still has on new generations of readers. I invite you to imagine yourself in a tapestry-hung great hall, among those medieval hearers. John Ridland's translation has made it easy to do that.

Maryann Corbett
Saint Paul, Minnesota

CONTENTS

Sir Gawain and the Green Knight

PART I

CHRISTMAS AT CAMELOT

After the siege and the assault had been exhausted at Troy,
    And the city had been broken to bits, and burnt to brands and ashes,
    The man that wrought that tragedy, by means of his treasonous works,
    Was brought to trial for treachery, truly the worst in the world.
    It was Aeneas the nobleman and his high-and-mighty kin,
    Who later oppressed many provinces, becoming overlords
    Of well-nigh all the wealth in the islands that lie away to the West.
    After that, Romulus, rich in rank, rushed swiftly off to Rome.
    He was the first with pomp and pride to build that city up,
10   And he named it from his own name, which now the place still bears;
    Tuscius turned to Tuscany, setting up dwellings to start with;
    Longbeard in Lombardy lifted up houses;
    And far across the French Channel, by a man named Felix Brutus,
    On many broad and sloping banks our Britain happily was
                  Created;
        To war, and woe, and wonder,
        By turns we have been fated;
        And here both bliss and blunder
        Have flourished or abated.
20 And after Britain had been founded by this noble lord,
    Bold men were bred up in it, who craved the clash of combat;
    Time after time, as the years turned, they stirred up many troubles.

And more amazing, marvelous things have come to pass in this country
Than in any other land I know of, since that ancient time.
But of all the kings that ever built in Britain, ruling here,
King Arthur was the noblest one, as I have always heard.
And therefore I intend to present an adventure, a true tale,
Which some of those among you may think more like a miracle,
An extraordinary adventure among the Arthurian wonders.
30   If you will listen to this tale, just for a little while,
I shall tell it to you right away, as I heard it in the court
                        Being told—

        Here written down in ink,
        A story strong and bold,
        Its letters truly linked
        In our Britain as of old.

★ ★ ★

King Arthur's court lay at Camelot as Christmastime was coming,
    Attended by many gracious lords, and the worthiest of knights—
    All the courtly brotherhood of the world-renowned Round Table—
40   With costly revelry carried on, and carefree entertainments.
    At times they conducted tournaments where many men would tilt,
    Jousting there most joyously, these knights of gentle birth,
    And afterwards rode back to court to sing and dance their carols;
    For there the festivities went on full strength for fifteen days,
    With all the meals and merriment that anyone could devise.
    Such clamorous and gleeful noise was glorious to hear,
    A delightful din all down the day, and dancing through the night,
    To the heights of happiness everywhere in the halls and in the chambers
    For those great lords and their grand ladies, whatever they liked best.

50 Indeed, with all the delight in the world, they were dwelling there together,

 The most noted knights that ever served, save for Christ himself,

 And the very loveliest ladies that ever lived on earth,

 And their king the handsomest ruler who ever had held court,

 For all these fair folk in that hall were in the flush that youth

Can give,

Since Heaven had blessed them most—

Their king superlative

In mind and will, his host

The hardiest troops alive.

60 While the New Year still was so very young it had only just come in,

 The court was served double helpings on the daises that day.

 From the moment the king had entered the hall in the company of his knights,

 After Mass had been celebrated by all with chanting in the chapel,

 Loud cries were being cast aloft, by clerics and by others.

 "Noël!" they shouted out anew, naming it over and over,

 And next the noble men ran out and passed their presents around,

 Crying loudly, "New Year's gifts!" and "Guess which hand it's in!"

 Busily bantering back and forth about the presents they gave.

 Ladies laughed out loud in sport even when they were losers,

70 And he who won would not be sorry, you may be sure of that.

 They kept on making all this mirth until it was time to feast.

 Then, after they had washed their hands, they went to their seats in order,

 The best-born always seated above, as it seemed proper to do.

 Queen Guenevere, the fairest of all, was set in their very midst,

 Taking her place on the high dais, with hangings all about:

 Fine silk draperies on the walls, and a canopy overhead

 Of excellent tapestry from Toulouse, and cloths from Turkestan,

 Embroidered, and among the threads the finest gems were set

 That could be purchased in those days, indeed at any price,

80   With many pence.

Breathtaking to behold,

With bright gray eyes she glanced;

A lovelier gem, we're told,

Never held men entranced.

But Arthur would not eat his meal until all the rest had been served,

So boisterous in his youthfulness, he was even somewhat boyish.

He liked his life to lie lightly on him, and two things he disliked:

Either to lie in bed too late, or to sit still too long,

Since his young blood and restless mind kept him busy all the time.

90 And also another inclination had lately become his custom:

For he in his high majesty declared he would not eat

On such a festive holiday before he had been told

A weird and wonderful account of some adventurous thing,

Of some amazing marvel that he might believe to be true,

About his ancestors and their arms, or other adventurers;

Or until some true knight sought from him a man of a similar sort

To join with in a jousting match, to lay themselves at risk,

A life for a life in jeopardy, the one against the other,

Allowing Fortune to favor one, to give that man the edge.

100 This was the custom for the king, when he was holding court,

At each and every splendid feast among his noble people

                         In the hall.

Proud in both face and figure,

He ruled them, standing tall

In the New Year, full of vigor,

Making merry with them all.

So there he stood, the spirited king, steadfast and masterful,

Chatting of gracious courtly trifles in front of the high table.

There good Sir Gawain was given a seat beside Queen Guenevere,

110 And Agravain of the Hard Hand sat on his other side,

  Both of them sons of the king's sister, his nephews, and trusted knights.

  At their table Bishop Baldwin sat, in the place of honor, by Arthur,

  And Ywain, son of Urien, shared the same platters with him.

  These seated on the dais were sumptuously served,

  And after them many trusty men, ranged at the long sideboards.

  Then the first course was carried out to the cracking sound of trumpets—

  Slung under every one of them, a brilliant banner hung;

  And a new noise of kettledrums combined with the noble bagpipes,

  Whose loud, wild, warbling notes wakened the hall's echoes,

120 So that many hearts were lifted high as the blasts of music touched them.

  Dishes came fast and furiously, piled high with many dainties,

  Such an abundance of fresh meats, laid on so many plates,

  That the servers had trouble finding room at everybody's place

  To set the silver platters down that held the broths and stews,

          On the cloth.

     Each lord took what he wished,

     None grudged him, none was loath;

     Each pair had a dozen dishes,

     Good beer and bright wine both.

130 But now I will say no more about the serving of their feast,

  For everyone must surely know that none would be left wanting.

  Another noise, entirely new, was nearing them in a rush,

  And this indeed would give the king permission to eat his dinner!

  For scarcely had the ringing trumpets ceased reverberating,

  And the first course had been served in the court to all, in order of rank,

  When in there burst through the hall door a horrifying figure,

  The tallest in his stature that ever stalked the earth;

  From his neck to his midsection so solid and squarely built,

  And his loins and limbs of such a length and also such a girth,

140   I wouldn't find it hard to grant he was genuinely half-giant!

         Nevertheless I must suppose he was actually a man,

         And quite the best looking of that bulk that ever could ride a horse;

         For although his body was so broad across the back and breast,

         Both his belly and his waist were slender, most becomingly,

         And every part of him in proportion completely followed suit

                         When seen.

               Men marveled at the hue

               That stained him with its sheen;

               Charging into their view,

150   He was—face and all—bright green!

     And his clothing, like the fellow himself, was all adorned in green:

         A straight, tight-fitting tunic clinging close about his trunk,

         With a handsome mantle over it, decorated inside

         With fur trimming around the edge where the elegant lining showed,

         Shining bright as ermine, and the same was seen in the hood

         That was tossed back, free of his locks, and lay across his shoulders;

         Snugly fitting stockings he wore, in that same shade of green,

         That hugged his calves, and he had strapped on bright spurs underneath

         Of shiny gold, over silken borders, which were richly striped,

160   And below his shanks he wore no shoes, as he came riding in.

         And all the rest of his vesture, truly, was also sparkling green,

         Both the bars running across his belt and the other brilliant stones

         That richly were arranged throughout his elegant array

         Over his person and his saddle, upon a silken backing.

         It would be tedious to tell you half the bright details

         That were embroidered over it, the birds and butterflies,

         With gay beadwork of bright green set in amidst the gold.

         The pendants of the horse's breastplate, the splendid crupper band,

         The studs on the bit, and all the metal, were coated with enamel;

170 The stirrups he stood up in were stained in the same way,

    And the saddlebows and saddle skirts were an identical shade

    That gleamed and glinted, all of them, and were inlaid with green stones.

    The horse the fellow rode on was colored the same as he,

          And grand:

      A green horse huge and thick,

      A steed hard to command,

      In its braided bridle quick,

      And well suited to the man.

  The knight was splendidly decked out, with all his gear in green,

180 And even the hair on his head agreed, matching that of his horse,

    The flowing locks were all fanned out, enveloping his shoulders.

    A mighty beard as big as a bush hung covering his chest,

    That, together with the splendid hair cascading from his head,

    Was clipped off in a circle at the level of his elbows,

    So the upper halves of his arms were hidden, precisely in the style

    Of a king's Cappadocian cape that closes around the neck.

    The mane of the man's magnificent horse looked very much like his own,

    Well curled and combed out carefully, containing many knots

    That were plaited in, with golden threads among the fair green hairs,

190 In every case one strand of hair aligned with another of gold.

    The tail of the steed and his topknot were twined in the same fashion,

    Both of them being bound about with a band of the brightest green,

    And studded with expensive stones all the way down to the dock,

    And then lashed tightly with a thong and an intricate knot on top,

    Where many brightly glittering bells of burnished gold were jingling.

    Such an animal on the earth, and such a worthy rider,

    Were never seen in that hall before by the eyes of any man

          Or lord.

      He glanced with lightning speed,

200   Those who saw him swore.

                            No man, they all agreed,

                            Might stand against his sword.

Nevertheless he wore no helmet, nor chain-mail hauberk either,

No steel plate over his breast and neck, nor any hint of armor,

Neither a shield nor a spear shaft with which to thrust or strike,

But in one hand, as a sign of peace, he held a holly bough,

That tree that burns the brightest green when all the groves are bare,

And in his other hand an axe, a huge and monstrous tool,

A brute of a battle-axe to describe in words, whoever might try.

210   The head was as long as an ell-rod, a yard and a span in length,

The spike on the tip was hammered out of green and golden steel,

The biting blade was burnished brightly, bearing a broad edge

As finely honed for slicing as a keenly whetted razor.

The shaft and hilt of the stout staff the grim man gripped it by

Were wound about with iron straps down to the butt of the helve,

And carved all over with green designs that were pleasingly engraved;

A leather thong wrapped around the shaft and fastened at the axe head,

Looping round and round the handle all along its length,

And many choice and splendid tassels, dangling off the strap

220   From buttons of a brilliant green, were richly braided there.

This splendid man reined in his horse, and entering the hall,

Drove straight up to the high dais, undaunted by any danger.

He hailed not one of them but stood and glared high over their heads.

These were the first words that he spoke: "Where," he said, "is the one

Who governs all this company? I would be glad to see

That lord with my own eyes, to speak with him who wears

                                  The crown."

                   On the knights he cast his gaze;

                   His eyes rolled up and down;

230   Paused; studied to appraise

          Who had the most renown.

For a long time all the men sat staring to behold this knight,

    For each one marveled to himself what such a sight might mean

    That a horseman, and his horse as well, should take on such a hue

    And grow as green as the grass grows, and even greener, it seemed,

    Than green enamel painted on gold, glowing even brighter.

    The servants who were standing by studied him, stalking nearer,

    With all the wonder in the world as to what he might want to do,

    For many marvels had they seen, but such as this one—never;

240   Therefore, people decided it was a phantom, a faerie trick;

    Which is why so many noble knights were afraid to answer him,

    And, wholly astounded at his speech, all sat as still as stones

    In a swooning silence through every corner of the resplendent hall.

    As if they had suddenly slipped asleep, the noise of their voices slackened

              Instantly:

        I think not all from fear,

        But some from courtesy—

        Let him to whom all defer

        Address him suitably.

250 Then Arthur, in front of the high dais, took in this awesome marvel,

    And greeted him in appropriate fashion, for he was never afraid,

    And said to him, "Sir, you are indeed welcome in this place.

    I myself am the head of this house, and Arthur is my name.

    Swing down lightly from your horse, and linger a while, I pray,

    And whatever it is you want from us, we shall find a little later."

    "No! so help me Him who sits on high," the knight replied;

    "To dawdle for any length of time in this dwelling was never my errand;

    But since your fame, good sir, is lauded loftily to the skies,

    And your castle and your knights in armor are reported to be the best,

260 The sturdiest men in steel gear that ever mastered steeds,

   The worthiest and manliest warriors anywhere in the world,

   Proven men to play against in every noble pastime,

   And this place renowned for courtliness—or so I have been told—

   Well, that, indeed, is what has brought me here at Christmastime.

   You may be certain by this branch of holly that I bear,

   I pass into this house in peace, not seeking any peril;

   Were I traveling with companions, in warlike fighting gear,

   I have a hauberk at my house and a helmet there as well,

   I have a shield and a sharp spear, shining splendidly,

270 And many other weapons at hand, that I know how to use;

   But since I wish no war with you, the weave I wear is softer.

   And now, if you really are as brave as all the warriors say,

   You'll grant me, out of your good grace, the simple game I seek,

           By right."

     Arthur made this reply,

     "If you, Sir Courteous Knight,

     Crave unarmed combat, why,

     You won't fail to find a fight."

 "No! I'm not asking for a fight, I tell you in good faith,

280 For sitting about on these benches I see only beardless boys.

   If I were buckled into my armor, mounted on my high steed,

   There's no man here to match me, their strength is far too weak.

   Therefore, all I crave in this court is a little Christmas game,

   Since it is Yule and New Year, and here are some lively lads.

   If anybody now in this house imagines himself so brave,

   To be so bold, and hot blooded, and so reckless in his head,

   That he'll dare stoutly strike a stroke and receive one in return,

   I shall present him with a gift, this gorgeous long-blade axe,

   This battle-axe, one of the heaviest, to handle as he likes,

290   And I shall endure the first blow, unprotected as I sit.

If any man is fierce enough to test what I propose,

Let him step smartly up to me and snatch hold of this weapon—

I'll quit my claim on it forever, let him keep it as his own—

And I will withstand a stroke from him, unflinching, on this ground,

So long as you grant me the right to deal him one in return,

To pay

Him back: yet give him a year,

Twelve whole months and a day.

All right now, quick! Let's hear

300   What anyone dares to say."

If he had astounded them at first, then now they were even stiller,

All the liegemen in that hall, the highborn and the lowly.

The horseman swiveled in his saddle, turning himself about

And roughly rolling his bloodshot eyes wildly around the court;

He arched his bristling eyebrows, which gleamed a vivid green,

And pointed back and forth with his beard, to see who would stand up.

When none would answer him man to man, he cleared his throat too loudly,

Drew himself up to his full height, and lorded it over them thus:

"What! Is this place King Arthur's house?" the haughty fellow scoffed,

310   "Which is continually praised throughout so many realms?

Where now is your arrogant pride, and all your mighty conquests,

Your great ferocity and fury, and your vainglorious words?

Now are the revelry and renown of the famous Round Table

Overturned with a single speech from one solitary man,

For you all cringe in your cowardice, without a blow being struck!"

With this he laughed at them so loudly their lord was stung to the core;

The blood shot suddenly into his fair face and his cheeks from shame

And disgrace.

He grew angry as the wind,

320
As all did in that place.
A king of the bravest kind,
He stepped up, face to face,
To that mighty man, and said, "By Heaven, sir, your request is daft,
And since you have asked for a foolish thing, it is fitting that you should find it.
I know of no knight here aghast at your vainglorious words.
Now hand me over your battle-axe, this minute, in God's name,
And I myself shall grant the favor that you've requested here."
He stepped up lightly to that knight and took it from his hand.
Then haughtily the other man dismounted onto his feet.

330
Once Arthur had the axe in hand, he gripped hold of the helve,
And fiercely brandished it about, preparing to deal that stroke.
The strong man stood in front of him, in all his towering height,
Taller by a head and more than any in the house.
With stern expression where he stood, he stroked and stroked his beard,
And with a countenance unmoved he pulled his collar down,
No more daunted nor dismayed at Arthur's sweeping strokes
Than if someone sitting on the bench had brought him a cup
Of wine.
Beside the queen, Gawain

340
Towards the king inclined:
"Please, sir—I speak it plain—
Let this contest be mine."
"If you are willing, my worthy lord," said Gawain to the king,
"To command me to step up from this bench and stand beside you there—
If I, without discourtesy, might leave my place at this table,
And provided that my liege lady shall not be offended—
I would come forward with this counsel, before your noble court.
For it strikes me as an unseemly thing, if the truth were to be known,
When such a haughty challenge is tossed aloft in your high hall,

350   For you to take it upon yourself, although your desire is strong,

While so many bold, brave warriors sit about you on the benches

That, under Heaven, I believe, there are none of more proven courage,

Nor fitter on the battlefield when fighting is afoot.

I am the weakest, I well know, and my wisdom is the slightest,

And the least loss of a life would be mine, were one to tell the truth.

Only inasmuch as you are my uncle am I to be praised;

There is no goodness in my body except that it bears your blood.

And since this ridiculous task is so far beneath your dignity,

And because I have been the first to ask, let it be assigned to me.

360   And if I speak out of order, let this noble court assign

The blame."

The courtiers whispered together,

Then all advised the same:

To rid the king of this blather

And give Gawain the game.

Then the king commanded the knight to rise from the bench and come to him,

And Gawain instantly stood up, and modestly made his way,

And kneeling down before the king, he took hold of that weapon.

Arthur graciously let him take it, and lifting up his hand,

370   He gave Gawain God's blessing, with good cheer bidding him

Be hardy in his heart and hand, both of them equally.

"Take care, Cousin," the king admonished, "that you carve just one cut,

And if you deal it deliberately, I truly do believe

That you will be able to withstand any blow he shall offer after!"

Gawain went up to the huge man, with his battle-axe in hand,

And the one who stood boldly waiting for him was not in the least dismayed.

The knight garbed all in green addressed Sir Gawain in this fashion:

"Let us go over our pact again, before we proceed any further.

First, I must request of you, sir, plainly, what is your name?

380   Tell me truly what it is, so that I may believe you."

"Truly, then," that good knight said, "Gawain is what I'm called,

Who now will offer you this blow, whatever may happen later,

And on this day twelve months from now, I will take a blow from you

With whatsoever weapon you wish—and not from any man else

Here below."

The other knight replied,

"Sir Gawain, on my soul,

I am greatly gratified

It's you who'll strike this blow."

390   "By God, Sir Gawain," the Green Knight said, "it's wholly to my liking,

That I shall be taking from your hand what I have asked for here.

And you have recited without hesitation, in precisely correct terms,

And clear through, all of the covenant I requested of the king,

Except that you must assure me, sir, and swear it on your oath,

That you will seek me out yourself, wherever you suppose

I may be found upon the earth, and there receive such a payment

As that you deal to me today before this noble court."

"Where shall I look for you?" Gawain asked, "Where is your dwelling place?

I have no idea where you live, I swear by Him who made me,

400   Nor, Knight, do I know your court, or even your proper name.

But direct me faithfully to your house, and tell me what you are called,

And I shall make use of all my wits to find my way to it,

And that, I swear to you, is the truth, upon my word of honor."

"That's quite enough in this New Year—no further oath is needed,"

Declared the gigantic man in green to the noble-hearted Gawain.

"If I can answer your questions truly, after I've taken your tap

And you have deftly struck me, then immediately I'll direct you

To my house and home, and I will tell you what is my proper name;

Then you may call on me, and thereby hold yourself to our pact.

410 And if I am unable to speak, then all the better for you,

You may linger on in your own land, and look for me no further!—so,

Don't hold back!

Take up your grim tool now,

And let's see how it hacks."

"I'll gladly show you how,"

And Gawain stroked his axe.

The Green Knight promptly prepared himself in position on the floor;

He bent his head a little down, uncovering the flesh,

And laid his long and lovely locks forward over the crown,

420 Leaving his naked neck exposed, before the business at hand.

Gawain took a grip on his axe, and gathered it up high,

He braced his left foot on the floor, a little ahead of the right,

And swiftly let the heavy axe swing down on the naked neck,

So that the sharp edge of the blade sliced into the man's bones

And sank clean through the shining flesh, cleaving it in two,

Until the edge of burnished steel bit straight into the ground.

The handsome head, lopped from the neck, dropped onto the floor,

Where many kicked at it with their feet as it was rolling about;

The blood was spraying out of the body, gleaming over the green.

430 Yet the fellow neither faltered nor fell, none the worse for all of this,

But stoutly he sprang forward at once upon his sturdy shanks

And violently he lunged to where the knights stood in their places;

He caught hold of his shapely head, and quickly lifted it up;

And after that he hurried back to his horse, and seized the bridle,

Stepped up into the steel stirrup, swinging himself astride,

And his own head dangling by the hair, he held in his other hand.

The rider settled himself securely, as well-seated in his saddle

As if no mishap had troubled him, although he sat in his place

With no head.

440   He twisted his trunk about,

That gruesome body that bled.

Many were filled with doubt

After all his words were said,

For now he was holding the head in his hand, upright on his palm,

     Aiming its face directly toward the nobles on the dais,

     And then it lifted its eyelids up, and stared with wide-open eyes,

     And out of its mouth it spoke to them, in words you now may hear:

     "Look to it, Gawain, that you are ready to go as you have pledged,

     And seek me faithfully, my man, until you find me out,

450   As you have promised in this hall, in the hearing of these knights.

     Make your way to the Green Chapel, I charge you, to receive

     A stroke just like the one you've struck—as you'll have well deserved.

     It will promptly be repaid to you on New Year's Day in the morning.

     Many people know me as the Knight of the Green Chapel;

     And so you will never fail to find me—if you seek me out.

     Therefore, come, or you'll deserve to be called a craven coward."

     With a violent yanking on the reins, he turned his horse around

     And hurtled out the hall door, holding his head in his hand,

     So fast that the fire flew from the flints struck by the horse's hooves.

460   Then to what country he returned, nobody there knew,

     Any more than they could know what place he had come to them from.

What then?

The king and Gawain shared

A laugh at him, a grin—

Yet openly they declared

It a wonder among men.

Although King Arthur, that gracious Lord, at heart was quite astounded,

     He let no semblance of this be seen, but spoke out confidently

And clearly, to the lovely queen, in a model of courtly speech:

470   "Dear lady, do not be dismayed at what we've seen today.

Mummery such as this is to be counted on at Christmas—

With the playing of our interludes, so we may laugh and sing—

Along with courtly carols that are danced by our knights and ladies.

Nevertheless, I may indeed address myself to my dinner,

For I have certainly seen a marvel—and that I can't deny."

He cast a glance upon Sir Gawain, aptly directing him,

"Now, sir, you may hang up your axe, it has hewn enough for now."

And it was displayed above the dais, hung on the tapestried wall,

Where all might look at it as a marvel, and stand in awe of it,

480   A testament to prove the truth of this wonder-making tale.

Then these two lords walked up together, seated themselves at table,

The king himself and the worthy knight, and eager servants brought them

Double dishes of all the dainties, a feast fit for a king,

Amid all manner of minstrelsy, as well as food—the both.

Thus they joyfully passed their time until the day was gone,

Forsaken.

Now, Gawain, pause and think:

Don't let your will be shaken,

Lest, terrified, you shrink

490   From this quest you've undertaken.

PART II | FROM CAMELOT TO HAUTDESERT

Thus Arthur was handed a New Year's marvel, a startling gift, first thing
    In the young year, what he'd been yearning for: to hear a boasting challenge.
    And though bold words had been lacking for him when the lords had gone to their seats,
    Now they were crammed with grim, weird work, their hands stuffed full of it.
    Gawain was glad enough to begin to play those games in the hall,
    But if the end should turn out heavy, you need not be surprised,
    For though men may be merry in mind when fortified with drink,
    A year rushes by so rapidly, and never brings back its like;
    The setting-out and the finishing-off seldom resemble each other.
500   And so this Yule passed over them, and the rest of the year followed,
    And each of the seasons in its turn pursued the one before:
    After the richness of Christmas come the crabbed weeks of Lent,
    That make a trial of our flesh with fish and plainer food.
    But then the weathers of the world battle it out with winter,
    The cold shrinks back down into the earth and the clouds lift to the loft,
    Brightness is shed as the shining rain in warm and warmer showers
    Falls on the fair flatlands below, where now the flowers are showing;
    Both open ground and groves of trees are clad in their green garments,
    Birds are abustle building their nests, and burst out boisterously
510   For the solace of the softening summer that will be following after

On the banks;

Blossoms break from their buds

By hedgerows rich and rank,

Then noble notes in the woods

Are heard as the birds give thanks.

Afterwards comes the summer season, breathing its soft breezes,

When the zephyr gently whistles through the seed grasses and herbs,

Wonderfully beautiful is the plant that burgeons out of doors

When drops of dew have drenched it and are dripping off the leaves,

520   And it enjoys the blissful gleaming beams of the bright sun.

But then the harvest hastens along, and urges the plant on,

Warning it to wax full ripe since winter is coming soon;

Autumn with its drought then drives the dust to rise in the air,

To fly up from the face of the earth, high into the heavens;

An angry wind falls out of the sky and wrestles with the sun,

The leaves are launched from the linden trees and light on the ground beneath,

And all the grasses are turning gray that were so green before;

Then every plant that first rose up now ripens until it rots,

And thus the old year rushes away in a river of yesterdays,

530   And winter winds itself round again, as is the way of Nature's

Passage,

Until the Michaelmas moon

Renews its wintry pledge.

Then Gawain must think soon

Of his arduous voyage.

Yet he remained until All Saints' Day, lingering with Arthur,

Who held a feast on that festival, for his nephew's sake,

With much extravagant revelry in the court of the Round Table.

All those chivalrous noble knights and lovely noble ladies

540   Were filled with great anxiety out of their love for that lord;

But nevertheless, they carried on, chatting of nothing but mirth.
Though joyless for that gentle knight, many of them made jokes.
But Gawain after the meal went up to his uncle, much oppressed,
And mindful of the ordeal ahead, he spoke to him openly,
"Now, liege lord of my life, I beg you, give me permission to leave.
You know the conditions of this contract; I would not care to tell
Its troublesome terms all over again—that would be trifling talk—
But tomorrow morning, without fail, I am setting off for the blow,
To seek the man in green, as God sees fit to be my guide."

550   At that the noblemen in the castle bowed their heads together,
Ywain, and Eric (son of Lac), and many another knight,
Sir Doddinal of the Savage Woods, and his cousin, Duke of Clarence,
Lancelot, and Lionel, and Lucan the king's butler,
Sir Boös, and Sir Bedivere, big men both of them,
And among the many other worthies, Mador de la Port.
All these companions of his court came nearer to the king,
To offer counsel to the knight, from concern they felt at heart.
Much grief and sorrow were secretly being suffered in the hall,
That a man as worthy as Sir Gawain should have to go on that mission,

560   Doomed to endure a dreadful blow, and never lift his sword
Up high.

The knight stayed always cheerful,
He said, "Why should I shy?
Whether Fate be fair or fearful,
What can one do but try?"

He stayed at Camelot all that day and dressed himself next morning,
Asking for his armor early, and all was brought to him.
First, a red carpet from Toulouse was spread out over the floor,
And a load of gleaming golden gear was piled on top of it.

570   The sturdy man stepped onto the rug and handled the steel pieces,

Clad in a doublet of costly silk woven in Turkestan
Under a well-made Cappadocian cape closed up at the neck
That was trimmed with an inner lining of bright white ermine fur.
Then they fitted the steel shoes onto the man's feet,
Lapped his legs around the shanks in greaves of well-shaped steel
With knee guards fastened on above, polished bright and clean
And tightly attached around his knees, tied on with golden knots;
Then some fine-looking cuisses, that cunningly were closed
Over his thick, brawny thighs, were tied around with thongs;

580   Next, his chain-mail hauberk forged from bright linked rings of steel,
Laced to a lovely material, enveloped the man's trunk,
And the shiny burnished sleeves of steel were fitted on both arms,
Together with strong bright elbow guards and gauntlets of plate mail,
And all the goodly gear for whatever use it could be to him

At last;

A rich coat over his armor,

Gold spurs proudly fixed fast,

His sure sword in its cover,

Girt with a silken sash.

590   When he had been buckled into his armor, his gear was glorious:
Even the least latchet or loop was alive with a gleam of gold.
So, dressed in armor though he was, he went along to hear Mass
Offered and celebrated for him in the chapel at the high altar.
After that he came to the king and his companions at court,
Where courteously he took his leave of all the lords and ladies,
And they kissed him and escorted him, commending him to Christ.
By this time Gringolet was groomed and girded with a saddle
That gaily gleamed with many fringes of gold that dangled down,
Everywhere studded with new nails that had been forged for the purpose.

600   The bridle was adorned with bars, bound with the brightest gold.

The decoration both of the breastplate and the superb saddle-skirts,
The crupper band, the caparison, all matched the saddlebows.
And all arrayed against a field of red were rich gold studs
That glittered and glinted as brightly as the sunlight gleaming off them.
Then Gawain picked his helmet up himself and kissed it quickly—
The steel was strongly stapled together, well padded on the inside.
High up on his head it rode, and was held by clasps in back,
Attaching it to the chain-mail neck-guard with a bright silk band,
Which was embroidered and adorned with the very choicest gems
610   Set on the edge of a broad silk hem with birds along the seams,
Parrots pictured preening themselves, among the periwinkles,
Turtledoves, and truelove knots in blossom, scattered so thickly
It seemed that many seamstresses had been sewing for seven winters
                In town.
          The band of gold, of greater
          Worth, circling his crown,
          Had diamonds of the first water,
          Both the clear kind and the brown.
And then they presented him his shield, the field of shining red,
620   Which had the pentangle painted on in the purest golden hue;
He drew it on by its crossbelt, which he tossed around his neck.
It suited this knight most fittingly, precisely as it should.
And why this pentangle should pertain so perfectly to that prince,
I am intent on telling you, though the telling makes me tarry.
It is a sign that Solomon set down a long time since
As a token of Integrity, which is what it rightly means,
For it is a figure of five points inscribed with a single line,
And each of the lines thus overlaps and locks onto the others,
And everywhere it runs endlessly (which is why the English call it
630   The Endless Knot, or so I have been told, throughout their land).

Now here is why it matched this knight, and matched his shining armor:
Since he was trustworthy in five ways, and five times in each way,
Gawain was widely known for his goodness, and, like refined gold,
Emptied of every sort of vice, and his virtues well defended

By moat.

The pentangle, painted fresh,

He wore on shield and coat,

This knight most true in speech,

His words of noblest note.

640   First, he was found without a fault in all of his five senses,
And secondly, his five fingers had never been known to falter,
And all his faith, upon this earth, was based in the five wounds
That Christ was dealt upon the Cross, as we are told in the Creed.
And wherever, in the midst of a melee, this man should find himself,
Against all other things, his steadfast thoughts were set on this:
That all his fortitude in fighting he took from the five joys
That the gracious Queen of Heaven had known, delighting in her Child.
And this was why the knight had arranged to have her image painted,
Most beautifully, on the inner surface of his shield,

650   So that whenever he glanced at her, his courage never failed.
The fifth set of five I find this man habitually practiced
Were his open Liberality, and beyond that, Brotherly Love,
His Purity and his Courtesy, which never went awry,
And Compassion, above all other points. And these pure, faultless five
Were wrapped more firmly around him than any other man.
Now all five sets of five, in fact, were fastened to this knight,
And each one firmly linked to the rest so that none ever came to a finish,
Fixed and established on five points, that never were known to fail,
And though never absolutely aligned, yet were never totally sundered,

660   Nor came to conclusion at any angle, as far as I can find,

Wherever you started tracing them, or glided to an end.
That's why the Endless Knot was fashioned on his shining shield,
Royally in reddish gold set against the red gules field.
This figure is called the Perfect Pentangle by the ones who know
The lore.

> Gawain, in bright array,
> Caught up his spear once more
> And wished them all good day—
> He guessed, forevermore.

670 With his spurs he prodded the steed along, and sprang out on his way
So forcefully that sparks flew up behind them from stones in the road.
All who watched that handsome knight sighed deeply in their hearts,
And everyone spoke the same sad thoughts softly to one another,
Since they cared so much for that lovely man: "By Christ, it is a pity
That he of all lords should be lost, who has led an exemplary life!
To find his equal upon earth, in faith, would not be easy.
It would have made more sense to have acted much more cautiously,
To have arranged for that noble lord to be appointed a duke.
To be a brilliant leader of men in the land would suit him well,
680 And that would have been much better than for him to be broken to nothing,
Beheaded by a macabre monster, out of arrogant pride.
Who ever heard of a king agreeing to such advice as this
From knights engaged in silly disputes over their Christmas games!"
How very much warm water there was that weltered from their eyes,
As that handsome-looking lord went riding away from their home
That day.

> He didn't hesitate
> But went swiftly on his way,
> By trails wild and desolate,
690 > As I heard the story say.

Now that he rode through Arthur's Britain, the southern realm of Logres,

Sir Gawain, in the name of God, decided this was no game.

Time after time, and all alone, he had to pass the night

Where what he found before him was nothing he liked to eat.

He had no companion but his horse, through the woodlands and the hills,

And not a soul to talk to but God as he traveled on his course,

Until at last he had made his way nearly into North Wales.

All the islands of Anglesea he passed by on his left,

And he traveled through those fords you find by the promontories there,

700   Over at Holy Head, until he had reached the other bank

In the wilderness of Wirral. Very few men lived there

Who were loved by either God or any person of good heart.

And always, as he pursued his quest, he asked the folk he met,

If they had ever heard any talk of a knight entirely green,

Or on any of the lands thereabouts was there a Green Chapel?

And all of them said nothing but "No!"—that never in their lives

Had any of them ever glimpsed a knight of such a hue

As green.

The ways he took were strange,

710   Past many a cheerless stream;

His spirits would often change

Before that chapel was seen.

Many cliffs he clambered over in those alien lands;

Having wandered far from his friends, he traveled as a stranger.

At every ford or running stream which the man was forced to cross,

Unless he had unusual luck, he found a foe before him,

And one that was so foul and fierce he was obliged to fight.

So many marvels that man met with there among the hills,

It would be tiresome were I to tell you even a tenth of them.

720   Some of the time he fought with dragons, other times with wolves,

Sometimes with hairy men of the woods who lived in the rugged rocks;

He battled both with bulls and bears, and other times with boars,

And giants that chased after him along precipitous cliffs.

And had he not been brave, long-suffering, patiently serving God,

Doubtless he would have been dead and gone, murdered many times over.

But though the fighting troubled him, the winter was far worse,

When cold clear water was shed on him from the clouds lowering above

And froze before it could even fall to the fallow, faded earth.

Nearly slain with the sleet he was, as he slept in his iron armor

730   More nights than enough, among the rough and naked rocks,

Where the cold creek ran clattering off the edge of the crest above,

Hanging high up over his head in rock-hard icicles.

Thus in danger and in hardship, through such perilous plights,

Across the countryside he rode, this knight, until Christmas Eve,

                Alone.

        The man, at Christmastide

        To Mary made his moan:

        Direct him where to ride,

        Guide him to someone's home.

740   Beside a mountain on that morning he rode magnificently

Into a deep, deep forest that was exceedingly wild,

High hills rising on either half and woods lying under them,

Hoary-gray gigantic oaks, a hundred altogether;

The hazel trees and hawthorn bushes tightly intertwined,

With rough and trailing rags of moss spread over everything,

And many birds there, far from blithe, perching on bare twigs,

Piteously piped their cries, from the pain of the piercing cold.

Sir Gawain riding Gringolet hurried on underneath

Through many marshes and miry bogs, one man all on his own,

750   And concerned for his religious duties, lest he should not be able

To observe the service of that Lord who on that very night
Was born of a maiden in order to quell our disobedience.
And therefore, sighing, he prayed aloud, "I beg of you, O Lord,
And Mary, the most merciful of mothers, and most dear,
Find me safe lodging in some house, devoutly to hear Mass,
And then your matins tomorrow morning, I meekly ask of you,
And to this purpose I promptly pray my *Pater* and my *Ave,*

> And Creed."
> He rode as he was praying,
> And wept for his misdeeds;
> He crossed himself too, saying,
> "May Christ's Cross grant Godspeed."

760

No sooner had he crossed himself, that man, no more than thrice,
Than he became aware, in the woods, of a building inside a moat,
Above a glade, set on a knoll, and locked in under the branches
Of many burly tree trunks which were growing outside the ditches:
A castle, quite the loveliest looking that ever a knight owned,
Pitched on a sort of paddock, with parkland all about,
Protected by a palisade of spikes set thick together
That ran for more than two good miles, enclosing a host of trees.
The knight regarded that stronghold from the outside, contemplating,
Watching as it shimmered and shone through gaps in the gleaming oaks.
Respectfully he removed his helmet, and solemnly he thanked
Jesus and St. Julian, both of whom are kindly,
For doing him the courtesy of listening to his prayer.
"Now for good lodging," the man pleaded, "I beg you both to grant me!"
Then he urged Gringolet along, prodding with gilt-spurred heels,
And found that he, entirely by chance, had chosen the main road
That would bring a knight directly up to the drawbridge end

770

780

> In haste.
> The bridge was tight atilt,
> The gates beyond, shut fast;
> The walls were stoutly built—
> They feared no wind's fierce blast.

The knight drew to a halt on his horse, and paused a while on the bank
    Of the deep, double-wide ditch they had dug to enclose the whole demesne;
    The wall plunged into the dark water, down to a wondrous depth,
    And then it lifted out of the moat to a lofty height above.
    It was constructed of hard hewn stone up to the top of the cornice,
790   Which jutted out under the battlements in the best defensive style.
    And watchtowers of the finest design were fashioned in between,
    With neatly cutout arrow loopholes readily shuttered and locked.
    That knight had never seen a better gatehouse fortification.
    And further inside the walls he could spot the main hall by its height;
    Turrets were erected between the ornate, thickset spires,
    Beautiful pinnacles deftly fitted together, exceedingly tall,
    Ingeniously crowned with well-carved ornamental caps,
    And chalk-white chimneys: he could make out crowds of them up there
    Topping the roofs of all the towers and gleaming shiny white.
800   There were so many painted pinnacles standing everywhere
    Among the flaring embrasures, so thickly clambering,
    That it looked as if the castle were clipped completely out of paper.
    The noble rider on his steed thought he'd be fortunate
    To make his way inside the walls, even just within the cloister,
    To find a harbor in that house for the holy day would be grand

> And pleasant.
> He called, and soon there came
> On the wall, faultlessly gallant,

A porter, who asked his aim,

810
                                    Saluting that knight errant.

"Good sir," said Gawain, "would you kindly carry a message from me

To the high lord of this household, that I ask shelter here?"

"Yes, by Saint Peter," the porter replied, "and I thoroughly believe

My friend, that you will be welcome here, to stay as long as you like."

The gatekeeper went away on his errand, and swiftly he returned,

Along with a number of folk to greet the knight hospitably.

They let the heavy drawbridge down, and walked out courteously,

And knelt down on their knees to him upon the cold hard ground,

To bid this same knight welcome in what they thought worthy style.

820
The broad gate opened wide for him, drawn back now all the way.

Politely he asked them all to rise, and he rode across the bridge.

Some hostlers held his saddle for him, assisting him to dismount,

And several strong men led his steed away to be well stabled.

Next, the knights and squires came down, out of the barbican,

To guide this great lord in with them, happily to the hall.

After he lifted his helmet off, some of them hurried to help,

Waiting upon that gracious lord, to receive it from his hands,

And along with it they took from him both his sword and his blazoned shield.

Then Gawain greeted graciously each of the noble knights,

830
And many proud men pressed forward there, in honor of that prince.

All fastened into his armor still, he was led by them into the hall,

Where a hearty fire was fiercely blazing in the open hearth.

Just then, the lord of all those people came down from his bedchamber,

To greet his guest on the floor of the hall with proper ceremony.

He declared: "You are welcome to do what you want, enjoy whatever you wish;

Everything here belongs to you, to command and rule as your own

                                    Home place."

                    "My thanks," said Sir Gawain,

"May Christ reward your Grace."
Like friends who meet again,
They joyfully embraced.

Gawain gazed at the gentleman who greeted him generously,
And thought this was a bold fellow, the one who owned the castle,
A massive manner of man indeed, and in the pride of life.
Broad and glistening was his beard, and reddish brown like a beaver;
Huge and strong, he took his stance upon his stalwart shanks,
His face was fierce as the fire, yet his style of speech was noble.
He was well suited, so it seemed—at least Sir Gawain thought—
To hold the lordship in this castle over such excellent knights.

850

The lord turned aside into a chamber, considerately commanding
That Gawain be assigned a servant, to attend him with respect,
And there were enough retainers at hand to do as their master bade;
They led Gawain to a cheerful room, where the bedding was rich and splendid:
The curtains of fresh and elegant silk, with bright gold sewn on the hems,
The bedcovers truly elaborate, with beautiful panel facings
Of shining white ermine above, embroidered down the sides.
The curtains ran along on cords, hanging from red-gold rings,
Tapestries from Turkestan and Toulouse were stretched on the walls,
And others of a matching sort were spread underfoot on the floor.

860

The knight was divested of his gear, with much good-humored banter,
His chain-mail shirt was stripped from him, and the rest of his bright garments.
Gorgeous, costly robes were quickly brought by his retainers
For him to consider, and change into, after choosing the best of them.
As soon as he had made his choice and wrapped himself in the robe,
One that suited him perfectly, skirts flowing past his knees,
The flush of springtime sprang in his face, and to tell the truth it seemed
To nearly everyone looking at him—all the most brilliant hues
Glowing from his handsome limbs under the clothes he wore—
That Christ had never made a more attractive-looking knight,

840

870   They thought.

         Whether from far or near

         He came, it seemed he ought

         To be a prince without peer

         In the field when fierce men fought.

A chair in front of the fireplace, where a charcoal fire was burning,

    Was pulled up for Sir Gawain, upholstered comfortably

    With cushions upon quilted seats that were skillfully stitched up,

    And then a gorgeous mantle was cast over the man's shoulders,

    Made of a brown, silky material richly embroidered over,

880   And warmly lined inside with fur from the very best of skins—

    The highest grade of ermine on earth—and his hood cut from the same.

    Becomingly and richly arrayed, he settled into his seat,

    Chafing his hands together briskly, and then his spirits mended.

    Without delay, on a pair of trestles a table was set up,

    Covered with a clean tablecloth that shone the clearest white,

    And on it a napkin and saltcellar and a setting of silver spoons.

    When he was ready, the man washed up, and sat down to his meal.

    The attendants served him respectfully, exactly as he deserved,

    With various excellent broths and stews, all seasoned delectably,

890   In double helpings, as was his due, and every kind of fish:

    Some of them were baked in bread, some, broiled over coals,

    Some were boiled, and some were stewed, made savory with spices,

    And all the sauces so subtly blended the knight was truly pleased.

    The fellow freely called it a feast, and said so over and over,

    Politely, while the knights all cheering him on in the same style,

                       Politely said:

        "Accept this penance, please;

        Soon you'll be better fed."

The man joked—at his ease—

900   For the wine had gone to his head.

Then questions and inquiries were put to him tactfully,

     Probing that prince, but delicately, and so discreetly addressed

     That he must admit without vanity that he belonged to the court

     That the lord Arthur, the noble-hearted, ruled over, he alone,

     Reigning majestically as the Royal King of the Round Table,

     And it was now Gawain himself, who was sitting in their house,

     Having come to them at Christmastime, as chance had brought it about.

     When the lord found out that he now held in his keeping such a knight,

     He laughed out loud at his good luck, he considered it so pleasing,

910   And all the men inside his castle felt quite as happy as he

     To make an appearance in Gawain's presence as promptly as they could,

     Since every excellence, all prowess, and the finest chivalrous conduct

     All appertained to this man's person, for which he was always praised;

     Before all other men on earth, his honor was the highest.

     Each of them whispered under his breath to his fellow standing by,

     "Now we shall see skilled demonstrations of sophisticated behavior,

     And learn the most faultless phrases to use in courtly conversation.

     We may pick up, without pressing him, how to speak in good company,

     Since luckily we find in our midst the father of fine breeding.

920   God has granted us His grace most generously, indeed,

     In allowing us to receive as our guest a model such as Gawain,

     At the time when all who rejoice at the birth of Christ will sit to sing

             His praise.

        Understanding of etiquette

        Is what this man will raise.

        Whoever listens should get

        Good lessons in love's ways."

After his dinner was finished, and the noble knight had risen,
Time had passed and the day drawn on until it was nearly night.

930 The chaplains had made their way along to the chapels and stood waiting,
Loudly ringing the bells for worship, as was their duty to do,
For the glorious service of evensong in the highest festival season.
The lord of the castle walked to his chapel, accompanied by his lady,
Who daintily entered her beautiful closed-in pew at the farther end.
Gawain happily hurried along, heading for the same chapel,
When the lord grabbed hold of a fold in his sleeve, and led him to sit in his.
Speaking to him familiarly, he called him by his name,
And said he was the most welcome man in the whole wide world to him.
Gawain thanked him earnestly, and the two embraced each other;

940 Then they sat soberly side by side as long as the service lasted.
When it was over, the lady grew curious, eager to look at that knight,
So out she came from her closed pew, with many fair women around her.
She was the fairest creature on earth, in her figure, and her complexion,
Her proportions and her coloring, her manners and her behavior—
More gorgeous even than Guenevere, was what Sir Gawain thought.
Out from the chancel into the church she went to make him welcome.
Holding her by the left hand, another woman led her,
Who was much older, indeed she seemed a venerable lady
And was treated with great deference by the knights all crowding around.

950 But these two ladies were most unlike each other in their looks,
For if the one was fresh and young, the other was yellow with age;
If the younger one was glowing all over, a rich and rosy red,
Then rough and wrinkled in loose rolls, the cheeks sagged on the other.
Kerchiefs covered with white pearls were worn by the young woman;
Both her breast and her bright bare throat were open to display
And shone more whitely than the snow that is shed on winter hills;
The other lady wore a scarf that draped across her neck,

And her black chin was muffled up with veils of chalky white;

Silk enfolded her forehead, which was wrapped up all around,

960   Framed by embroidered hems and fine-stitched latticework of lace,

So that no part of that lady was bare, except for her black eyebrows,

And her two eyes, and the nose between them, and her naked lips;

And these were so ugly to look upon, the eyes so runny and bleared

That God knows, nobody in the world might call her a handsome lady!

Instead—

Short, thick about the waist,

Her buttocks bulged and spread;

More delectable to the taste

Was the lady whom she led.

970   When Gawain glanced at that fair lady, who gazed with favor on him,

At once he excused himself from her lord, and walked across to the two.

He paid his respects to the elder woman, bowing low to her,

Then he lapped the lovelier lady about, though lightly, in his arms,

Kissing her in the courtly manner, and conversing in knightly style.

They begged the favor of his acquaintance, and instantly he offered

To be their true and faithful servant, if that should be to their liking.

The two women took him along between them, talking, and leading him

To a chamber, and sat him down by a fireplace, first of all calling for

Spiced cakes, along with excellent wine mulled in the finest way,

980   Which men unsparingly sped to bring—and brought more whenever they asked.

In friendly fashion, over and over, the lord leapt to his feet,

And many a time reminded them all to keep on making merry.

Ceremoniously he pulled off his hood, and hung it high on a spear,

Challenging everyone present to gain the honor of winning it:

It would go to whoever gave them the most to laugh at, at Christmastime:

"And I shall be trying, upon my faith, to contend for it with the best,

With the help of my friends, before I will ever give this garment up."

Thus with laughing, lighthearted words the lord himself made merry,
In order to gladden Sir Gawain's heart in the hall that night with the games

990
He led,

And when the time was right,

"Torches!" the Master said.

Sir Gawain said "Good night,"

And straightway went to bed.

On the morning after, as everybody remembered this was the time
When God was born to die for us and so take on our fate,
Joy welled up in every dwelling on earth for our Lord's sake.
So did it there upon that day, through many delicacies:
For both the breakfast and the main meal, cleverly cooked-up dishes
1000
Were laid invitingly out on the dais by sterling serving men.
The venerable lady sat in the highest place of honor,
The lord politely took his place beside her, I believe.
Gawain and the fair young lady were sitting side by side,
At the middle of the table, where the food came first, as always,
And after, was passed around the hall, as it was right to do,
Until everyone present was properly served, according to his rank.
There was so much food, there was so much mirth, so much delight and joy,
That for me to relate the whole of it would be a wearisome task—
If I, for instance, took great pains to tell it point by point.
1010
But all the same, I know Gawain and the charming lady by him
Together were taking such comfort in each other's company
Through their discreet conversation, in the private words between them
Of clean-minded, courtly dalliance, free of all filthy phrases,
That their playful pleasure surpassed, in truth, any other nobleman's who

Was there.

Trumpets blared, kettledrums beat,

Bagpipes warbled their airs.

Each tended his own delight,

And those two tended theirs.

1020 All around, much merriment was made, through that day and the next,

And the third day, equally crowded, thronged in on the two before.

The celebrations on Saint John's Day were glorious to hear,

And brought the holidays to an end, as everyone knew they would.

The guests were to go in the gray morning, departing at dawn next day,

And therefore some of them stayed awake, amazingly, drinking wine

And dancing and singing their favorite carols, almost incessantly.

At last, when it had grown very late, they began to take their leave,

Each of the visitors setting out to make his own way home.

But when Sir Gawain began to say goodbye, the good host seized him,

1030 Led him into his own chamber, sat him down by the fire,

And there detained him while he thanked him enthusiastically

For the credit his presence had conferred on him and all his house,

The honor he'd paid by visiting now, at this high tide of the year,

Embellishing the fame of his court with his gracious company.

"I know, sir, that, as long as I live, I shall be a better man

For having Gawain as my guest, in the season of God's own feast."

"I thank you, sir," replied Gawain, "but in good faith it is yours:

All the honor is yours alone—may the High King repay you—

For I, my lord, but serve at your bidding, to act at your behest,

1040 As I am wholly bound to do, whether for high or low,

By rights."

The lord then took great pains

To detain that worthy knight.

To him replied Gawain:

There was no way he might.

At that the lord inquired of the knight politely, could he say

What dreadful deed had driven him at this dearest time of year

To ride away from his king's court, so urgently, all on his own,
Before the holidays wholly passed, to go traveling from his home?
1050 "To tell the truth, sir," said the knight, "what you have said is true,
A momentous and an urgent mission has taken me from that court,
For I am summoned to go in person and seek a certain place—
I do not know in what direction to ride in order to find it.
But I would not wish to be anywhere else but there on New Year's morning
For all the land in Arthur's Britain, so help me our Good Lord!
Therefore, sir, I must ask you this, as politely as I can,
That you might tell me truthfully: Have you ever heard any tales
About the so-called "Green Chapel"—where on earth it stands,
And about the knight who is colored green, and keeps it in his charge?
1060 There was established by solemn pact between us an appointment
For me to meet him at that landmark, if I should live so long.
And now it is lacking but a little of that same New Year's Day,
And I would like to lay eyes on that lord, if God would let me do so,
More gladly, by the Son of God, than possess any worldly goods!
And so, indeed, with your permission, I have no choice but to leave,
For there now remain a bare three days to go about this business,
And I would as soon fall stricken by death as fail to fulfill my mission."
Then laughingly the lord spoke out: "Now you have no choice but to *linger!*
For I shall direct you, in ample time, to your appointed place.
1070 Let the whereabouts of the Green Chapel trouble you no longer,
For you, my good man, will lie in bed, completely at your ease,
As late as you like on that first day of the year, and then go riding
And come to that landmark by mid-morning, to do whatever you're there
                About;
         Stay on till New Year's Day,
         Then rise up and ride out.

My man will lead the way—

Not two miles by that route."

Then Gawain was as glad as could be, and he laughed happily,

1080   "Now I thank you above my thanks for all your other favors.

Now that my search is almost over, I shall indeed, as you wish,

Dwell here awhile, and in everything else I will do as you see fit."

Then the host seized hold of him again, and sat him down beside him,

And called for the ladies to be brought in, to please his guest the better.

Off by themselves, what a time they had, the four of them together!

The lord let loose, for friendship's sake, such hilarious jests,

That he seemed like a man going out of his mind, not knowing what he might do.

And then he spoke these words to the knight, in fact, he shouted aloud:

"You have agreed to do whatever I may assign to you.

1090   So will you, at this very moment, hold yourself to this promise?"

"Yes, sir, for certain," said Gawain, who was known for his truthfulness,

"As long as I'm lodging in your castle, I'm bound to do what you ask."

"You've had a hard journey," said the lord, "traveling from far away,

And lately staying up all night with me, you're not yet fully recovered,

Either in sustenance or in sleep, and that I know is true.

So you will linger in your loft, and lie sleeping at your ease

Tomorrow until it is time for Mass, and after that, eat your meal

Whenever you like, along with my wife, and she will sit with you

And comfort you with her company, till I return to court.

1100   You stay,

        I'll rise before first light

        And hunt throughout the day."

        Gawain, as befits a knight,

        Bowed "Yes," in his courtly way.

"Just one more thing," the master said. "Let us make an agreement between us:

Whatever I may win in the woods, it shall belong to you,

While any misfortune you encounter, I shall take in exchange.
Sweet sir, shall we make a swap like this—to answer honestly,
Regardless what either of us receives, the worse or the better lot?"

1110   "By God," said Gawain, that good man, "I agree to it completely,
And I am as glad as I could be that you've come up with this game."
"Let someone bring us beverage, and this bargain will be sealed,"
The lord of that company exclaimed, at which they laughed together.
Chatting of elegant trifles, they drank, and reveled without restraint,
These courtly lovers, both lords and ladies, for quite as long as they liked,
And next, with manners in the French style and many fair-spoken phrases,
They stood up, and they milled about, and confidentially whispered,
Kissed one another courteously, and at last they took their leave.
With many light-footed serving men, who led them with gleaming torches,

1120   Each noble lord was brought at last to his chamber and his bed

So soft.

Yet before they went to sleep,
They rehearsed their compact often.
The lord of those folk could keep
The fun and games aloft.

PART III | THE HUNTING

Early, before the day had dawned, the guests were rising from bed,
    Those who were eager to get on the road called aloud for their grooms,
    Who hustled along in a great hurry to saddle up their steeds,
    Gather their tackle and gear and pack them, trussing them into their bags.
1130   Those of highest rank dressed first, and, well arrayed for riding,
    Leapt up lightly onto their horses, catching hold of the bridles,
    And every man of them went his way, wherever he had to go.
    The well-beloved lord of that land was not the last of them
    To be arrayed for riding out, along with many retainers.
    After he had listened to Mass, he bolted down a bite,
    And with bugle calls he hastened away toward the hunting field.
    Before a gleam of daylight glimmered anywhere over the land,
    He and his knights on their high steeds already were starting out.
    The expert handlers of the hounds leashed them together in pairs,
1140   Unlatched and threw open the kennel doors, and called the dogs outside;
    Boldly on the bugles they blew a triplet of three long notes.
    The hounds in turn set in to baying, raising a frightful racket;
    Any dogs who'd gone chasing ahead were chastised and turned back.
    A hundred of these huntsmen set forth, I've heard, the best that could
                                    Be found.
            Keepers went to their posts,

Handlers unleashed their hounds;
Through that forest the bugle blasts
Raised a great clamor of sound.

1150   The first outcry from the questing pack set the wild creatures quaking;
The deer were driven into the valley, frenzied with their dread,
Or hied themselves to the high ground, but there they were forcefully met,
Blocked, and turned back by the ring of beaters, shouting harshly at them.
These let the harts with their antlered heads pass freely through their ranks
And also the fierce fallow bucks, with the broad beams of their horns,
For the noble lord had forbidden them to be hunted in the close season,
Declaring that no man should arouse any of the male deer.
The red deer hinds, however, were halted with shouts of *Hey!* And *Ware!*
And the fallow does with a great din were turned to the deep gullies.

1160   There you might see, as they slipped and slid, the slanting flight of arrows;
At every bend beneath the trees, a shaft rushed whistling by
And bit deep into brown hide with its full broad arrowhead.
What a noise! They shrieked and bled, dying along the banks,
And always the scenting hounds were chasing headlong after them,
While mounted hunters with high-pitched horns hurried along behind,
Making such cracking echoing cries as if the cliffs were splitting.
Whatever wild thing went rushing free, escaping the archers' shots,
Was pulled down and then slashed apart at the receiving station
Once they'd been harried up on the heights and herded down to the waters

1170   By expert men at the lower posts who knew what they needed to do,
And the great greyhounds that were so huge they could seize the deer alive
And pull them down as fast as a man could turn and look at them,

Right away.
The lord dashed left and right,
On and off his horse all day.

Thus to the dark of night,
Blissful, he led the fray.
In this style the lord was enjoying his sport by the edge of the linden woods,
And Gawain, that good fellow, lay in his luxurious bed,
1180   Quiet and snug, away in there, until daylight gleamed on the walls,
Under a clean bright coverlet and curtained all about.
And as he slipped in and out of sleep, he heard a soft small sound,
A wary rustling at his door, which was opened stealthily;
At this he lifted his head clear from under the bedcovers;
He raised a corner of the curtain cloth a little bit,
And cautiously peeked out through the gap to see what it might be.
It was the lady of the house, the loveliest to behold,
Who drew the door closed secretly and silently after her,
And headed for the bed—the knight was in a predicament,
1190   And cunningly laid his head back down, pretending to be asleep.
And she stepped forward furtively, and stole to where he lay,
There she lifted the curtain up, and crept in under it,
And seated herself down daintily beside him on the bed,
Prepared to linger as long as it took, to see when he woke up.
The knight lay low, though, keeping silent and still, for a long time,
Mulling it over in his mind what this circumstance might mean,
Or amount to. It was a marvel, he realized at once.
"All the same," he reflected, "It would be more appropriate
To find out what the lady wants by having a talk with her."
1200   So he made a show of waking up, stretching, and turning towards her,
And when he unlocked his eyelids, he pretended to be amazed,
And with his right hand crossed himself—as if a prayer could keep
Him safe.
Her chin and cheek shone bright,
White and red, half and half;

Her demeanor was polite,

Her small lips pursed to laugh.

"Good morning to you, Sir Gawain," the lovely lady said,

"You are a careless sort of sleeper, if someone can slip in here!

1210 Now you are captured in a flash! Unless we arrange a truce,

I shall bind you in your bed, you may be sure of that."

Laughingly the lady launched these jibes against the knight.

"Good morning, lovely lady," Gawain answered cheerily,

"You shall use me as you wish, at which I am well pleased,

For I surrender immediately, and cry aloud for Mercy!

And that's the best thing I can do, I judge: I have no choice."

Thus he bantered back at her with much light-hearted laughter.

"But, lovely lady, if you would only grant me your permission,

And now release your prisoner, and tell him to get up,

1220 Then I would bolt straight out of bed and dress myself much better;

I would be all the more comfortable in conversation with you."

"No, no, indeed, my handsome sir," the sweet thing answered him,

"No, I can't let you out of bed. I've something better in mind:

I'll tuck you in as tight on the other side as you're tucked on this,

And then I'll have a little chat with my knight whom I have captured,

For I know perfectly well, I tell you, that you are Sir Gawain,

And you are held in such high regard that everywhere you ride

Your honor and your courtliness are given such gracious praise

By lords and ladies both, in fact, by everyone alive.

1230 And now you're here, I'm happy to say, and we are all on our own;

My lord and his huntsmen have ridden off on their horses, far away,

The other men are asleep in their beds, and so are my women-in-waiting.

The door's drawn all the way shut and fastened with a sturdy latch;

And since I have in my house the lord that everyone adores,

I'll make the most of my time with him, for as long as it may last,

This tête-à-tête.

Indeed, you are welcome to me,

And I beg you, fill your plate.

From sheer necessity

1240 To serve you is my fate."

"In good faith," Gawain answered her, "that would be a generous gift,

Though I am not at all the man that you are speaking of—

To receive so rich an honor as you have offered me;

I'm too unworthy a fellow, as I'm all too well aware—

By God, I'd be extremely glad, if you should think me fit

To devote myself, by word or deed, to you, to serve or speak

To please you as you most deserve; it would be the purest joy."

The lively lady then replied, "In good faith, Sir Gawain,

If the excellence and the prowess that so please all the others

1250 Were slighted or denied by me, it would be simply rude.

But there are ladies enough in the land who'd be even more delighted

To have you, dear sir, in their hold, as I now have you here,

To dally with your delightful words, amusing them playfully,

To find some comfort for themselves and cool their love longings,

Than to own however much treasure or gold they happen to possess.

But I—for which I praise the Lord who upholds the sky above us—

Have wholly in my hands what every one of them desires,

Through grace."

She made him such great cheer,

1260 And was so fair of face,

The knight's speech was sincere

As he answered her each phrase.

"Madam," the merry man declared, "may Mary well repay you,

For I have found, in all good faith, your generosity noble;

Other men have performed good deeds when guided by other folk,

But the honor that has been offered me is nothing I have deserved;
The honor thus is owed to you, for the goodness of your heart."
"By Mary," the noble lady countered, "I conceive it otherwise:
For if I were the worthiest of all the women on earth,

1270 And all the wealth in the whole world were mine to hold in my hands,
And I could bargain to win the chance to choose myself a lord,
For all the virtues I have found in you, my knight, right here,
Of handsomeness and graciousness and cheerful disposition—
Which I have heard about before, and now know to be true—
There would be no man on this earth I would choose ahead of you."
"Never say so, noble lady, for you have chosen much better.
Yet I am proud of the high value that you have placed on me,
And as your servant, I sincerely accept you as my sovereign,
And I declare myself your knight, and may Christ reward you well."

1280 They chatted like this about many things until mid-morning had passed,
And always the lady made it appear that she loved him very much.
The man conducted himself defensively, yet in the courtliest fashion;
And although she was the loveliest lady he could remember seeing,
He brought much less of love with him because of the fate he would meet

So soon—

The blow he'd be receiving,
And all that must be done.
When the lady spoke of leaving,
He agreed to it at once.

1290 Then she gave him a warm "Good day," and with it a laughing glance,
And standing up, she surprised him with these sternly spoken words:
"Now may He who blesses every speech repay you for this pleasure!
But whether you really are Gawain is a question in my mind."
"Why would that be?" the man inquired with utmost eagerness,
Afraid that he had somehow failed in the forms of his utterances.

But the lady reassured him, saying, "Bless you," and "This is why:
Gawain is held in such esteem, and very rightly so,
Since the model of courtliness is contained, complete, in his own person.
He could not have lingered as long as this, lightly beside a lady,

1300   Without requesting a kiss from her, out of simple courtesy,
Or at least by some small trifling hint dropped in at the end of a speech."
Then Gawain said, "So let it be done, exactly as you wish,
For I shall kiss at your command, as it falls to a knight to do,
And all the more, lest he displease you, so plead it now no further."
With that she moved even closer to him and caught him in her arms,
And bending lovingly down to him, she gave that lord a kiss.
Each of them graciously commended the other to Jesus Christ;
She went by herself out through the door without making a sound,
And he prepared to rise at once, and hurried as fast as he could;

1310   He called out for his chamberlain, selected his set of clothes,
And left his room, when he was dressed, and went cheerfully down to Mass,
And after that, along to his meal, which was fitly waiting for him,
And passed the day, till the moon rose, in merriment and sport
And mirth.

No man has ever known
With two women of such worth,
The young and the elder one,
More pleasures on this earth.

And all this time the lord of the land is bent upon *his* sport,

1320   In the woods, hunting, and on the heath, chasing the barren hinds;
Such a number of them he slew by the time the sun slanted down,
Of does and other female deer, that to count them would take too long.
Then eagerly all the folk flocked in, en masse, at the end of the day,
And quickly they made a quarry pile of all the deer they'd killed.
The highborn walked up to it first, with men enough for the task,

Gathered together the deer in the heap that were most filled out with fat
And neatly dismembered them, cutting them up as the rites of the task demand:
They examined them at the first assay, sampling a few of them;
And they found at least two fingers of flesh on even the leanest ones.

1330   They slit the slot at the base of the throat, and seizing hold of the gullet,
Shaved it clean with a sharp knife, and tied it in a knot.
Next they severed the four limbs, and then stripped off the hide;
They broke the belly open for the bowels to be lifted out,
Skillfully, so as not to loosen the binding of the knot.
They gripped hold of the deer's gorge, and readily separated
The gullet from the windpipe, and then tossed the guts away.
Then they cut free the shoulder joints, using their sharp knives,
Drawing them out through a little hole, to leave the sides intact;
Next they opened the breastbone and divided the breast in two.

1340   After that they began on the gorge, setting to work at once,
Ripped it open rapidly, up to the fork of the forelegs,
Emptied the neck offal out, and then, proceeding correctly,
All the membranes along the ribs were speedily cut loose.
So too, they cleared in the proper way the ridge bones of the back,
Trimmed them all the way down to the haunch, so it all hung together,
And lifting up the whole of the loin, they hewed it off right there—
And that, to give it its proper name, is the "numbles," I believe,

In a hind.
By the fork of the thighs they sliced

1350   The loose skin off behind,
Dividing it lengthwise
By the backbone, to unbind.

They hewed the head and neck off the hind together in one piece,
And then they swiftly split the sides away from the bones of the spine,
And the scrap they call "the raven's fee" they cast off into a thicket.

They drilled a hole through each thick flank, in the region of the ribs,
And hung the haunches of venison up, hooked by the hocks of the legs,
For each man to receive his prize, the share that fell to him.
To feed their hounds, the hunters spread on a hide from the noblest beast,
The liver and lights, the leathery tripe, the lining of the paunch,
1360   And bread that had been bathed in blood, all mingled in together.
Trumpets boldly blew the blasts for "Capture!" The hounds bayed,
And every man took up his share of the meat and headed home,
Sounding the bugle stridently with many drawn-out notes.
By the time that daylight was over and done, the party had settled down
Inside the lovely castle where Sir Gawain had been waiting

Quietly,

With a cheerful bright fire burning.

As the lord came in to see,

1370   Gawain met him returning.

They were glad as men could be.

Then the lord commanded all his men to assemble in the hall
And told his ladies to come down, from upstairs, with their women.
Before these folk on the lower floor, he ordered his serving men
To fetch his portion of venison and spread it out before him.
Then graciously he called Gawain, in the spirit of their game,
And directed his attention to the tally of full-grown beasts,
Showing him the shimmering rolls of flesh shorn from the ribs:
"And how does this play please you? Would you say I've earned some praise?
1380   Have I thoroughly merited your thanks for my skill at hunting the hinds?"
"Yes, indeed," the other said, "for here is the finest harvest
That I have seen in seven years, in the bitter season of winter."
"And all of it I give to you, Gawain," said the fellow then,
"For in accord with our covenant you can claim it as your own."
"That is the truth," the knight replied, "And I say the same to you:

What I have honorably won within the walls of this house,

Indeed with equally good will, it must belong to you."

He grasped the fellow's handsome neck and folded it in his arms,

And kissed him quite as courteously as ever he could devise:

1390   "There you take all that I have won; I achieved nothing else,

I hand it over completely, as I would if it were more."

"It's good," the good man said to him, "And therefore, many thanks.

However, it might be even better if you would let me know

Where you have won this self-same wealth, by what wit on your part?"

"That was not in our compact," he said, "you may question me no further,

For you have taken what's owed to you; you may expect no more to be

                Your due."

          They laughed and they made merry,

          With praise words free and true.

1400   To supper they went in a hurry

          For dishes dainty and new.

And afterwards the two men sat by the chimney in the chamber,

Servants brought cups of the choicest wine, recharging them over and over,

And again, amid their jesting, they agreed that in the morning

They would fulfill the same compact that they had made before:

Whatever good fortune was their lot, they would exchange their winnings,

Whatever new thing they might claim—at night when they met again.

They bound themselves to this covenant in front of all the court—

The beverage to seal the pledge brought forth at once with jests—

1410   Then graciously they each took leave of the other at the last,

And both men hurried off to their rooms at once and went to bed.

As soon as the morning cock had crowed and cackled only thrice,

The lord had bounded out of bed, and so had each of his knights,

And when they had gone to morning Mass and duly dispatched their meal,

The hunting party took to the woods, even before day broke—

> To the chase.
> Loudly, huntsmen with horns
> Flew through the fields apace,
> Unleashing among the thorns

1420
> The hounds in a headlong race.

Soon these gave tongue and the search was on, along a wooded marsh;
The huntsmen urging those hounds on that had first picked up the scent.
They shouted at them excitedly, raising a clamorous noise.
The other hounds, hearing this hubbub, hastened to join the fray,
And fell on the trail as furiously, forty of them at once.
Then such a babble of ear-splitting barks rose up from the gathered dogs
That the rocky hillsides rang with the uproar echoing all around.
The hunters cheered them on with both their voices and their horns;
Then the whole assemblage moved as one, swinging swiftly down

1430
Between a pool in the forest and a most forbidding crag.
On a rocky knoll beside a cliff, at the very edge of the marsh,
Where the rough rocks had tumbled down in a jumble of debris,
They set to scenting out the prey, with the men in hot pursuit.
Casting about, they surrounded both the crag and the wooded knoll,
The men in a ring until they could tell for certain it was within—
The beast that thus had been announced by the baying of the bloodhounds.
Then the beaters thrashed away at the bushes, and challenged him to come out;
And he broke cover menacingly, straight across the line of men:
One of the cruelest of wild boars, he bolted out of cover,

1440
Who long before had left the herd on account of his great age,
For he was an enormous beast, the most massive of all boars,
And the way he snorted was terrifying: many were dismayed,
For at his first onrush, he threw three good men down in the dirt
And sprang away at breakneck speed, though not harming any others.
They hallooed "Hi!" at the top of their lungs, and shouted out, "Hey! Hey!"

They held their horns up to their lips and blasted the notes for "Rally!"
Many encouraging calls came out of the mouths of men and hounds,
That rushed on after this fearsome boar, crying out with their clamor
> For the kill.

1450
> > Many times he stood at bay,
> > Maiming the pack at will.
> > He hurt some hounds, and they
> > Whimpered and yowled and yelled.

Then the men with bows pressed in around to shoot at the savage boar,
They loosed their arrows at the beast, and they hit him over and over,
But the arrow points were blunted by the tough hide of his shoulders
And none of them would bite through into the bristles of his brow;
The smoothly shaven arrow shafts split apart, shivered and splintered,
The heads bounced off again and again, wherever they hit the brute.

1460
When the blows began to injure him with their incessant strikes,
Then, frenzied into a fury to fight, he charged at the men around,
Savagely wounding the ones in his path where he went speeding forth;
Many were terrified at that, and faltered, drawing back.
But the lord of that land on a lively horse dashed ahead after him,
Like a bold knight on a battlefield, he blew a bugle blast,
Called his men back to rally again and rode through the brushwood thickets
Pursuing this wild swine until the sun had begun to set.
All day long with deeds like these they drove on after him,
While in the castle our gracious knight was reclining in his bed,

1470
Sir Gawain, happily at home, under the covers so splendidly
> Hued.
> > The lady didn't forget him
> > And came with her salute;
> > Quite early, she was at him
> > To change his attitude.

She came to the curtain around his bed and peeped in at the knight.

    Sir Gawain was the first to speak, to welcome her courteously,

    And she replied to him in turn, in her most fervent words,

    Sat herself softly by his side, and broke out in sudden laughter,

1480   And with an amorous, gracious look, she scolded him like this:

    "Sir, if you really are Gawain, I have to think it's a wonder

    That a man well known for always acting with propriety

    Is so unable to understand the rules of polite behavior,

    And when someone bothers to point them out, you cast them from your mind!

    You have totally forgotten what I taught you yesterday

    By a truer lesson than any that I could put to you in words."

    "What lesson is that?" the man inquired, "Indeed I have no idea.

    If this fault that you declare is true, the blame must all be mine."

    "And yet I taught you this about kissing," the fair one then explained,

1490   "Where acquiescence is plainly given, quickly to claim a kiss

    Is becoming behavior in every knight who practices courtliness."

    "Enough of that!" the man exclaimed, "My dear, enough such talk,

    For that is a deed I dare not do, for fear I should be denied.

    Were I turned down, I would indeed be wrong to have offered it."

    "My faith," the merry wife remarked, "you would never be turned down.

    You are strong enough to enforce your will, if you should feel the urge,

    Were any woman so boorishly bred that she would try to deny you."

    "Well yes, God knows," Gawain replied, "What you say may be true,

    But threats are thought to be barbarous in the country I come from,

1500   And likewise any gift that is not given willingly.

    I am entirely at your command, to kiss me when you like,

    You may seize me when it pleases you, and let go when you think right,

                    Without delays."

        The lady then bent down

        And graciously kissed his face.

They talked away, expounding
On love, its griefs and grace.
"I would like to learn from you, good sir," that worthy lady said,
"So long as you will not be angry, what reason there might be
1510   That a man as young and vigorous as you are at this time,
So courteous, and so knightly, as you're widely known to be—
And since, of all chivalric deeds, including the lore of arms,
The chief one to be practiced is the loyal sport of love;
For, in telling of the difficult quests undertaken by true knights,
This is the title, sign, and text from which their works are drawn:
How lords for the sake of their true loves have risked their very lives,
And have endured (and all for love) the dolefullest of days,
And afterwards avenged themselves with their valor, banished care,
Bringing bliss to a lady's bower, through their openheartedness—
1520   And you are known as the noblest of all the knights of our time,
Your fame and honor travel before you everywhere you go,
And I have sat beside you here, on two distinct occasions,
Yet I have never heard one word from that handsome head of yours
That had a thing to do with love in any way at all.
And you, who are so courteous and so careful to keep your vows,
You ought to be eager to instruct a young thing in its ways,
And teach her some of the secrets of the art and craft of love.
Or—What! Can it be you are ignorant, despite your high repute?
Or do you think I am too dull for courtly conversation?
1530   For shame!
I come alone here, sit,
To learn about love's game.
Do teach me some of it
While my lord's away from home."

"In good faith then," Sir Gawain said, "And may God give you grace!
    Great is the happiness I feel, and the pleasure for me is great,
    That so worthy a noblewoman as you should deign to visit me here,
    And bother yourself with so wretched a man, amusing yourself with your knight,
    By showing him any kind of favor—it gives me the greatest comfort.

1540   But to take the travail upon myself of expounding upon true love,
    And to touch the themes of that thorny text, telling tales of men in arms,
    To you, who I know very well wields greater skill by far
    In that art, by at least a half, than a hundred of such men
    As I am, or shall ever be, as long as I live on earth,
    Why, it would be manifold folly, lady, upon my plighted word.
    I would perform whatever you wish, as far as is in my power,
    As I am duty bound to do, and I will evermore
    Act as a faithful servant to yourself, so help me God!"
    Thus that lady made trial of him, tempting him over and over,

1550   Trying to win him to woo, or woe, or whatever she had in mind,
    But he fended her off so fairly that there seemed to be no fault,
    And nothing wicked on either half, so they felt nothing at all
                    But delight.
        They flirted and they played;
        She gave a kiss, polite;
        Their parting words were said;
        She left, and all was right.
Then the man bestirred himself and rose, and went along to Mass,
    And after that their dinner was prepared and lavishly served.

1560   The knight played love games with the ladies lightheartedly all day,
    But the lord was dashing back and forth, galloping over his lands,
    Pursuing his ill-fated swine, which bolted along the bankside
    And bit the best of his hunting dogs, cracking their backs in two.

He lurked in the brush at bay until the bowmen broke his stand
And forced him out, and into the open, no matter what he could do,
So fiercely the arrows flew at him, when the men had gathered around.
Yet still he caused the most fearless of them to flinch from him at times,
Until at last he was so worn out that he could no longer run,
But hastily, as best he could, beat a retreat to a hole

1570   On a ledge beside a rocky bank above a running brook.
He put the bank behind his back and began to paw the ground—
The froth was foaming ferociously from the corners of his mouth—
As he stood whetting his white tusks. The men surrounding him,
No matter how bold and brave, had begun to tire of the hunting trip,
Of trying to hurt him from far off, yet none would dare close in

For dread:

He'd savaged so many before,

All feared what lay ahead—

That his tusks would slash some more—

1580   Ferocious and out of his head,

Until the lord of the castle charged up, spurring his horse along,
Saw the boar biding his time at bay while his men were standing by,
And swung down lightly to the ground, leaving his charger behind.
He drew his bright sword from its sheath, and strode in with all his strength,
Splashing swiftly through the ford to where the fierce beast lurked.
Warily the wild thing watched the man with weapon in hand,
The bristles on his ridge rose up, and he snorted so threateningly
That many feared for their lord's life, if he got the worst of it.
Then the swine charged against the man, straight at him where he stood,

1590   So the lord and the boar fell over together in a tangled heap
In the swiftest part of the stream. But the animal had the worst of it,
For the man had aimed at him accurately, as they first clashed together,

Set his sharp point firmly in the slot at the base of the throat

And drove it in up to the hilt, so it sundered the heart in two,

And the snarling beast yielded up his life, and was quickly swept downstream,

Aside.

A hundred hounds seized the boar

And fiercely bit his hide;

Men brought him back to shore

1600   And the dogs made sure he died.

Then there was blowing of blasts for "Capture!" shrilly on many horns,

And each hallooed at the top of his voice as loudly as he could;

The hounds were baying at that beast, as bidden by their masters,

The ones who had been huntsmen-in-chief on that long and difficult chase.

Then a man who was wise in all the crafts that are needed in the woods

Started skillfully to unlace the carcass of the boar.

First of all he hewed off the head and set it aside up high,

And then he rent him roughly apart along the ridge of the spine,

Pulled the bowels out in a braid and charred them on red-hot coals,

1610 Blending them with bits of bread as a bonus for his hounds.

And after that, he sliced the flesh into bright broad slabs of meat,

And lifted the edible entrails out, as was right and proper to do,

And next he fastened the two halves back together as one whole

And finally, over a stout pole he hung them, securely tied.

Now with that same swine swaying from it, they rapidly made for home.

The head of the boar was borne along in front of the master himself

Who had, through main force of his hand, killed the creature in the ford,

His foe.

Until he saw Gawain

1620   He thought it a long road.

He called, and Gawain came

Promptly for what he owed.

The lord burst out in boisterous speech, and merry jubilation
　　When he laid eyes on Sir Gawain, and full of joy he spoke.
　　The good ladies were summoned and came, and the household company gathered.
　　He showed them the shields of wild boar meat and told them the whole tale,
　　Of the bulky breadth and length of the beast, and its ferocity,
　　And the war he waged with the wild swine, after it had fled in the woods.
　　The other knight most courteously commended his host's deeds

1630　　With praise for his high excellence, of which this had given proof,
　　For such a brawny beast, indeed, the valiant visitor said,
　　And such great flanks of swine flesh he had never seen before.
　　Then they held up the head between them, which the knight praised lavishly,
　　Pretending he found it even more loathsome, to laud that lord the more.
　　"Now, Gawain," that good man declared, "this catch is all for you,
　　According to our binding compact, as you most certainly know."
　　"That is the truth," the knight replied, "and it is as surely true,
　　That all I have won I shall give to you, again, as by my oath."
　　He clasped that nobleman round the neck, kissed him once, courteously,

1640　　And then immediately he served him the same reward again.
　　"Now we are even," the bold knight said, "once more at eventide,
　　In all the covenants that we made, since the day I first came here—
　　　　　　　　　Tit for tat."
　　　　　The lord said, "By Saint Giles,
　　　　　You're the best man I have met.
　　　　　You'll be rich in a little while
　　　　　If you can trade like that!"
Then servants lifted the table boards, and laid them on the trestles,
　　Tossed the tablecloths over them, and lit the brightest lamps

1650　　Which kindled and blazed along the walls, as torches made of wax
　　Were set in place by some of the men, while others served in the hall.
　　Much joyful noise and merriment sprang up in that great room

Around the open fire on the floor, and taking various forms

During supper and afterwards, as many noble folk

Performed old Christmas carols and the newest songs-and-dances,

With all the well-mannered sort of mirth that anyone could dream up.

And always our amiable knight was accompanied by the lady.

Such a kindly eye on that chivalrous man she continually cast

With sly and stealthy sidelong glances designed to please that stalwart,

1660   That the knight was not only taken aback, but angry with himself,

Although, because of his good breeding, he could not gruffly rebuff her,

But dealt with her in a delicate fashion, however his deeds might be

Misconstrued.

They dallied in the hall

As long as they felt the mood;

"To my chamber!" the lord's call

Brought them where its chimney stood.

And there they drank and chatted a while, and decided once again

To set themselves the same conditions, on what was New Year's Eve.

1670   And the knight begged leave of his noble host to ride away in the morning,

For it was nearly the time appointed when he would have to leave.

The lord attempted to change his mind, urged him to lengthen his stay,

And said, "As I am a true knight, I give you my word of honor,

You shall find your way to the Green Chapel, and attend to your affairs,

My dear Gawain, at New Year's dawn, long before nine o'clock.

Therefore, you should lie in your bed upstairs, and take your ease,

While I am hunting in the woods, and holding our covenant

To exchange whatever I win with you, when I have come back home.

For I have tested your temper twice, and I find you trustworthy;

1680   'Third time,' they say, 'is the best throw': you should think of that tomorrow.

Let us make merry while we may, and give our minds over to joy,

For indeed a man can take hold of Sorrow whenever he wishes to."

This agreement was quickly granted, and Gawain persuaded to stay.
The drink was cheerily brought to them, and they were led to their beds
With torches bright.

Sir Gawain lay and snored,
Unstirring, snug all night;
Eager to hunt, the lord
Was dressed before daylight.

1690 After taking Mass, he and his men had only a morsel to eat.
The morning was a merry one: the lord called for his mount,
All the nobles attending him when he went riding out
Were dressed and ready on their steeds outside the gates of the hall.
The earth was wondrously fresh and fair, for the frost lay clinging to it;
The sun rose, spreading a fiery red across a rack of clouds,
And then with the brightness of its beams drove the clouds out of the sky.
The handlers had unleashed their hounds when they came to the edge of a woods,
The rocky hillside in the forest rang with the blare of their horns:
Some of the dogs picked up the trail to where the fox was waiting,

1700 And worked across it back and forth with their customary craft.
A small hound cried, catching the scent, the huntsman called to him,
The rest of the pack followed his lead, hastening, panting hard.
They ran forth in a rabble rout, close on the fox's trail,
And though he frisked and scampered ahead, they soon picked up his scent,
And when their eyes caught sight of him, they set off in hot pursuit,
Vilifying him unmercifully with a fearsome angry clamor.
Trickily he twisted and turned through many troublesome thickets,
Doubled back and stopped, listened, sidling along the hedges,
And at the last by a little ditch leapt over a low fence

1710 And stole out stealthily, running a rough path at the forest border.
And he had half-escaped from the hounds in the woods by his wiliness

When, before he knew it, he stumbled onto a well-kept hunting station
Where three great greyhounds lunged at him, straining at the leash,

All fierce.

He blenched, and quickly whirled,

Turned boldly to reverse;

With all the woe in the world,

To the woods he took his course.

Then was it worthwhile living on earth, to hearken to the hounds!

1720   When all the pack had met up with the fox, and they mingled all together,
Such curses they called down on his head at the very sight of him
As if the cliffs that clambered above had come clattering down in heaps!
Here he was hallooed after when the hunters on horseback spied him,
In great commotion greeted by them, chastised and castigated,
Denounced and threatened in their shouts, and all cried at him, "Thief!"
And hounds in relays chased at his tail, so he couldn't pause for breath.
Often when he broke for the open, they raced out after him,
And often they reeled him in again, though Reynard was so wily.
And yes! he led them in a string, the lord and all his men,

1730   In a line along the tops of the hills, until mid-afternoon,
While the noble knight lay sleeping healthfully in the lord's great house,
Cozy inside the rich bed-curtains, on the chilly morning.
But the lady, out of her longing for love, would not let herself sleep late,
Or the purpose that she nursed in her heart might be blunted by delay.
She rose up rapidly from her bed and made her way to his,
Wearing a handsome mantled robe that hung all the way to the floor
And was fully lined with the finest fur, on skins trimmed to perfection;
No wimpled coif upon her head but a fretwork of well-wrought gems
That were set in clusters of twenty in a net that held her tresses.

1740   Her lovely face and open throat were naked to the eye,

Like her breast which was laid bare in front, as also was her back.
She slipped in through his chamber door, and shut it after her,
Swung a window open wide and, calling out to the man
Right away, she rallied him in pleasing, teasing words
Of cheer:
"Ah, man! How can you sleep?
The morning is so clear!"
He had been drowsing deep,
But her words had reached his ear.

1750 That noble knight lay muttering, in the sway of disturbing dreams,
As a man who was sorrowing, set upon by many oppressive thoughts—
How Destiny on the very next day would deal his fate to him
When he must travel to the Green Chapel to meet that man at last
And wait there for the stroke of his axe without any more debate.
But when that comely creature came, he recovered the use of his wits,
And, startled out of his dreams, he woke and answered her at last.
The lady in all her loveliness came laughing sweetly to him,
She bent low over his handsome face and gave him a dainty kiss.
He welcomed her politely, in a well-bred cheerful manner,
1760 But seeing her look so radiant, and so gloriously attired,
So flawless in her features, and the perfect flush of her face,
Joy came swelling strongly up and warmed him to the heart.
With friendly smiles they spoke together, softly but cheerily,
So that all was bliss and *de bonheur* that broke between them both,
And delight.
They chatted merrily;
Their words were gay and bright.
But between them stood great peril
Unless Mary watched her knight.

1770   For that priceless princess kept after him so, pressing him thick and fast,

        Entreating him on to the end of the thread, to the point where he must decide

        Either to help himself to her love, or else reject it rudely.

        He felt concerned for his courtliness, not to act like a churlish boor,

        But more for the guilt his soul would carry, if he should commit a sin,

        And play the traitor to his host, the lord who owned that house.

        "God shield me," said the man to himself, "that this shall not befall!"

        And so with a little flirtatious laughter he parried and pushed aside

        All the sweet speeches of special affection springing from her lips.

        Then the lady addressed the knight: "Sir, you will be to blame

1780   If you will not give your love to the woman that you are lying beside,

        Who is, before all others on earth, the most wounded in her heart—

        Unless you have a love of your own, a mistress whom you prefer,

        A lady to whom you have plighted your word, and are fastened so firmly to,

        That you never may undo that knot—and that's what I now believe!

        And if that's the case, then tell me so, I pray you truly now,

        For all the loves alive in the world, don't hide the truth from me,

                            Through guile."

                The knight said, "By Saint John,"

                Smiling a pleasant smile,

1790   "In faith, though, I have none,

                Nor shall have for a while."

   "Those are the words," said the woman then, "that are the worst of all,

        But I am answered, that is certain, though it pains me to the heart.

        Come kiss me now in courteous fashion, and I shall be on my way.

        I must only grieve for the rest of my life, as a woman who loves too much."

        Sighing she swooped down over him, and sweetly kissed his lips,

        And then she moved away from him, and said as she stood up,

        "Now, my dear, since we must part, do me at least this favor,

Give me some token as a gift—your glove or some little thing,

1800   That I may remember you, my man, to lessen the pangs of grief."

"I surely wish," Sir Gawain said, "that I had with me in this land

The dearest thing that I own in the world, to offer you for your love,

For you have so many times, indeed, deserved, to tell the truth,

Much more in the way of a reward than I can ever give.

But to deal you out in return for your love some piece of paltry value—

It would not be worthy of your honor to offer you such a thing,

To give a glove as a meager keepsake, a goodbye gift from Gawain.

For I am here on a dangerous mission in a strange and alien land,

And I brought no men with bulging bags of valuable things,

1810   Which makes me most unhappy, lady, because of my love for you,

But every man must do as he can. I ask you, take it not ill,

                         Nor frown."

           "No, lord of such high honors,"

           Said the lady in linen gown,

           "Though I have nothing of yours,

           You shall have something I own."

She offered him a costly ring that was cast out of red gold,

With a stone like a staring, fiery eye mounted high on it

Which gleamed at him with glancing beams as bright as those of the sun—

1820   You can be sure that it was worth a huge amount of wealth.

But the knight could only say *No* to it, and directly he declared,

"God knows, I wish no gifts from you, fair lady, at this time;

Since I have none to give in return, I will take none away."

She pressed it on him more urgently, but he still refused the gift,

By swearing swiftly, on his honor, that he would not accept it.

And she was sorry that he rejected it, saying so to him,

"If you are turning down my ring because it appears too costly,

And you would rather not feel yourself so greatly obliged to me,

Then I shall give you my girdle-sash, since it is worth much less."

1830   She quickly undid the belt she wore fastened around her waist,

Tied with a knot about her tunic, under the bright mantle.

It was woven out of green silk, the edges trimmed with gold;

Every bit of it was embroidered, ornamented by hand;

And this she offered to the man while playfully she implored,

That even though it was worth so little, would he be willing to take it?

At first he insisted that he would not be willing on any account

To take either gold or other treasure, before God gave him grace

To achieve the end of the adventure that he had chosen to take.

"And therefore, I pray that you will not be offended at what I've said,

1840   But let your persistent urgings rest, for I promise you I never

                         Can consent.

            I am deeply in your debt,

            Your kindness is well-meant,

            And through cold and heat I'll yet

            Remain your true servant."

"Now maybe you are refusing this silk," the lady suggested to him,

"Because it's so little in itself? And so indeed it appears—

Look! It is slight, a trifle, and worth even less than that.

But a person who knew the properties that are knitted into it

1850   Would appraise it at a much higher price, I have to think—perhaps.

For whoever girds himself about with this sash of lacy green,

As long as he keeps it tightly fastened, tied around his waist,

There is no warrior under heaven can hew him down to earth,

For he cannot be slain by any stratagem in the world."

This set the knight to pondering, and the thought came into his heart,

It could be a jewel against the jeopardy he had been allotted

When he arrived at the Green Chapel, to be checkmated there.

If he could slip through and not be slain, such sleight of hand would be splendid.

So he patiently put up with her pleading, permitting her to speak,

1860   And she pressed the belt upon him again, urging it earnestly,

Until he agreed to accept it, and surrendered with goodwill,

While she begged him, for her sake, to never let it be seen,

But to promise to hide it from her lord. The knight agreed to that:

No one should ever know of it, except the two of them,

No matter what.

He thanked her, truly glad

In both his heart and thought.

By then the lady had

Thrice kissed the hardy knight.

1870   And after that she said goodbye, and left him lying there,

Since she saw she would receive no more amusement from that man.

When she was gone, Sir Gawain rose, and dressed himself at once,

Richly arrayed for the coming day in a splendid set of clothes.

He put the love-lace safely away that the lady had given him,

Hiding it, true to her command, where he could find it again.

Then he decided to make his way rapidly to the chapel,

Where he privately approached a priest, and prayed him then and there

To listen to his confession and to teach him to live better,

In order that his soul be saved, when he would leave this world.

1880   There he shrove himself all clean by confessing his misdeeds,

Both the major and the minor ones, and begging the Lord for mercy;

He prayed the priest to provide him with his absolution for all,

And he absolved him absolutely, sending him out as pure

As if Doomsday had been due to fall upon the following morning.

And then Sir Gawain made himself more jolly among the ladies,

Joining in happy dancing songs, and every kind of glee,
Than he had ever done before that day, to the dark of night—

Sheer bliss.

Everyone said, delighted:

1890   "This merriment of his—

He was never so excited

Since he came here, as this."

Now let us leave him in that harbor, where love can lap him about.

The lord of the castle was still in the field, pursuing his pleasure there,

And now he had headed off the fox that he had followed so long;

As his horse was leaping over a hedge, he sought to spot the villain

Where he'd heard the hounds in hot pursuit chasing after him full speed.

Reynard at last came into view, trotting through a tangled thicket,

And all the rabble in a rush racing after at his heels.

1900   The lord kept his eye on the wild thing, and warily waited for him,

Then drawing out his shining sword, he aimed it at the beast,

Who swerved away from the sharp blade, and would have scampered off,

But a scenting hound seized hold of him, before he gave them the slip,

And directly in front of the horse's hooves the pack all fell on him,

Catching the wily one by the throat and raising an angry ruckus.

The lord jumped quickly down from his horse and snatched hold of the fox,

Swiftly ripped him away at once out of the mouths of the hounds,

Held him high up over his head, hallooing lustily

While all around the grim fierce dogs kept baying up at him.

1910   The other hunters came hurrying in, many of them with horns,

Blowing the "Rally!" call as they should until they could see their lord.

When his noble company had assembled, all of them in one crowd,

Those who had brought their bugles along were blowing them at once,

And all the others, who had no horns, were hallooing as loud as they could.

They made the merriest clamor and baying that any hunt ever heard,
A resounding uproar there they raised for the soul of poor Reynard—

A din!
The hounds had their reward,
They were stroked and patted; then,
1920   The huntsmen took Reynard
And stripped him of his skin.

And with that they headed home at once, for night had nearly fallen,
Trumpeting their triumph proudly on their strident horns.
The lord at last leapt lightly down at his beloved house,
Where he found a fire on the open floor, and the fellow standing beside it,
Gawain, the good and noble knight, as happy as could be—
Among the ladies and their love he had taken great delight.
He was wearing a garment of rich blue silk that reached all the way to the ground;
His outer robe fitted perfectly and was lined with a soft fur,
1930   His hood, cut from the same cloth, was hanging from his shoulders,
And both were trimmed around the edge with ermine or the like.
Forward he stepped to meet his host in the middle of the floor,
And greeted him, full of merriment; courteously he said,
"Now this time I shall be the first to carry out our compact,
Which we have speedily affirmed, sparing nothing in our drink."
Then he embraced the noble lord, and kissed the man three times
With all the relish and liveliness that he could muster up.
"By Christ!" the other knight then said, "You have been a lucky man
In bargaining for this merchandise, if you've bought at a good price!"
1940   "Never you mind about the price," Gawain replied at once,
"As long as the goods I deliver to you have been truly and fairly paid."
"By Mary," said the lord of the house, "my goods lag far behind,
For I have been hunting all day long, and nothing to show for it
But this foul-smelling fox's pelt—the Devil take such goods!—

Since that's a poor return to pay for three such precious gifts

As you have pressed upon me here, with these three hearty kisses,

So good."

"Enough," said Sir Gawain,

"I thank you, by the Rood."

1950   And the lord told how he'd slain

The fox, as there they stood.

With much mirth and much minstrelsy and all the food they wanted,

They made themselves as merry then as any men might do,

Joined by the laughter of the ladies, and many jesting words.

Sir Gawain and the noble lord could not have been more glad,

As if the crowd had all gone mad, or everyone was drunk.

Both the lord and his retainers kept on making jokes,

Until they were looking at the hour when they must separate,

And the two of them must part and go their ways to bed at last.

1960   Then bowing deferentially the noble knight took leave,

First of the lord, to whom he poured out generously his thanks:

"May the Highest King reward you for the fine sojourn I've had,

And the honor you have done me through these high festivities!

I'll offer you my services for those of one of your men,

If you approve, for, as you know, I must move on tomorrow,

If you will let me take one man to instruct me, as you pledged,

The way to the Green Chapel, where, as God wills, I'll receive

On New Year's Day the judgment He will bring down as my fate."

"In good faith," his good host replied, "I will do so willingly.

1970   All that I ever promised you I am ready to fulfill."

He assigned a servant there and then to set him on the road

And conduct him over the downs and on, so that he without delay

Might ride there, taking the shortest route they could follow through the woods

And groves.
The lord thanked Gawain gladly
For the honor that he gave;
Then of the ladies, sadly
The knight must take his leave.

With great distress and kissing, he conversed with the two women,
1980   And pressed them to accept his hearty, overflowing thanks,
And promptly they replied to him in exactly the same tones,
As they commended him to Christ, with melancholy sighs.
And after that he most courteously took leave of the household staff;
Each of the servants that he greeted, he gave him special thanks
For his dutifulness, and his kindnesses, and the trouble he had taken—
For all of them had been so busy about him, serving him;
And every one was as sorry now to say goodbye to him
As if they had served that gentleman in honor all their lives.
Then, with attendants carrying torches, he was led to his room.
1990   And they cheerfully conducted him to his bed, to take his rest.
Whether he slept there soundly or not, I would not dare to say,
For he had many things on his mind, if he wanted to, to hold

In thought.
So let him lie there still;
Nearby is what he sought,
And if you'll for a while be still,
I'll tell how it turned out.

PART IV | THE MEETING

Now New Year's Day was drawing nigh, and the night before it passed,
Daylight was driving the dark away, as the Lord above commands.
2000 But a wild weather was working up in the world outside their doors:
Keenly the clouds cast a bitter cold down onto the earth,
With enough of a cruel wind from the north to torment the naked flesh.
The snow fell snittering sharply, it was stinging the wild beasts;
The whistling wind whipped down upon them shrilly from the heights,
And filled the hollows of every dale full up with heavy drifts.
The knight was listening closely to this as he lay awake in his bed,
And though he locked his eyelids shut, he got very little sleep:
From each cockcrow throughout the night he could tell what hour it was.
Hurriedly he rose from his bed before the day had broken,
2010 For there was light enough from a lamp that was glowing in his room.
He called out to his chamberlain, who promptly answered him;
He bade him bring his chain-mail shirt, and saddle up his horse.
The man obediently got up, and fetched the garments for him,
And started to dress Sir Gawain, in the most resplendent style.
First he put on his warmest clothing, which would ward off the cold,
And next he brought the armor out that had been carefully stored:
Both the belly piece and all the plate had been buffed and was shining clean,
The rust on the rings of his costly chain-mail shirt had been rubbed off,
And all gleamed freshly as when first forged, for which he was eager to thank

2020   Them all.

               When he had donned each piece—

               All of them polished well—

               Unmatched from here to Greece,

               He bade, "Bring my steed from his stall."

While the noble knight was being arrayed in his most sumptuous clothes—

    The surcoat draping over his armor adorned with the pentangle badge

    Stitched onto velvet, framed around with precious, potent stones

    Inlaid along the embroidered seams, setting it off so well;

    On the inner side the coat was richly trimmed with beautiful fur—

2030   Nor did he leave the lace behind that had been the lady's gift;

    That present Gawain did not forget, for the good of his own self.

    After he had belted the sword above his powerful haunches,

    He wrapped the love-token carefully two times around his waist;

    Quickly and delightedly, he wound it about his middle.

    The girdle woven of green silk well suited that splendid man,

    Against the royal red of the cloth, which looked rich enough in itself.

    But he was not girding himself with this because of its costliness,

    Nor out of pride in its shiny pendants, however polished they were,

    Nor even for the glittering gold that glinted upon the fringe,

2040   But in order that he might save his life when he was obliged to submit,

    To face without dispute what he would take from the sword's or knife's

                       Quick stroke.

               Once the brave man was set,

               He hurried out and spoke

               His thanks to all he met,

               Of all the noble folk.

Then Gringolet was readied to ride, which was an enormous horse

    And had been stabled comfortably, in snug and secure style:

    That horse wanted to gallop now, due to his fit condition.

2050 The knight walked out to where he stood, and gazed on his glistening coat,
      And soberly he said to himself, swearing it on his oath,
      "Here inside this moat is a company setting their minds on honor:
      May joy come to the lord who maintains and manages them all;
      And as for the delightful lady, may she have love in her life!
      If out of charity they can receive and cherish a guest so kindly,
      And offer such hospitality, may the Lord provide reward
      Who holds the heavens up on high—and also the whole household!
      And if I should stay alive on earth, for even a little while,
      I would quickly pay you some recompense, if I were able to."

2060 And he stepped up into the stirrup, swung his leg astride the horse;
      His servant handed him his shield, which he settled on his shoulder,
      And he dug his spurs into Gringolet, kicking his gilded heels;
      The horse started forward over the stones, no longer standing still,
                              To prance.
                    The man was mounted by then
                    Who bore his sword and lance.
                    "This castle I commend
                    To Christ against mischance!"
      The drawbridge was lowered for him to pass, and the broad gates in the wall
2070 Were unbarred, swung open on either side, all the way back on both halves.
      The knight crossed himself rapidly and passed along the planks,
      Thanking the porter who kept the gates, who knelt before the prince—
      He gave the knight "Good day" and prayed that God would save Gawain,
      Who went on his way, accompanied by only a single guide
      To teach him the turns by which to reach at last that perilous place
      Where he was fated to receive the grievous, fearful stroke.
      They bent and stooped beneath bare boughs along the hillside slopes;
      They climbed and clambered below the cliffs where the cold was clinging close.
      The heavens were holding high above, but were threatening underneath;

2080 The mist was mizzling on the moor and melting on the mountains.
Each of the hilltops had a hat, a huge mantle of mist.
The brooks were boiling and foaming over, breaking above their banks,
White water shattered against the sides, where they made their way downhill.
The route was wildly meandering that they followed through the woods,
Until it would soon, in that winter season, be time for the sun to break
From night.
They stood on a high hilltop;
On all sides snow lay white;
The guide with him called, "Stop!"
2090 Abruptly, to the knight.
"For I have brought you hither, sir, at the appointed time,
And now you are not far away from that noteworthy place
That you have sought and asked about so very particularly.
But I shall tell you the truth, my lord, since now I know you well
And you are one man on this earth whom I regard most highly:
If only you'd act on my advice, you would be much better off.
The place you are pressing forward to is held to be perilous;
A man lives in that wasteland who is the worst in the world,
For he is strong and stern and grim and loves above all to smite.
2100 In his massiveness he is more of a man than any on Middle Earth,
His body is bigger than four of the best and biggest knights to be found
In Arthur's house—he is bigger even than Hector or any other—
And he is in charge of all mischance that happens at the Green Chapel,
For nobody passes by that place, however proud in arms,
But he will batter him to death by dint of the strength of his hand,
For he is a man without restraint, and is utterly merciless:
Whether it be a churl or a chaplain that's riding by his chapel,
Whether a monk, or a priest who says Mass, or any manner of man,

He thinks it as fine to murder him as to stay alive himself.

2110   Therefore I have to say to you, as sure as you sit in your saddle,
If you go there, you will be killed, if that knight has his way—
Trust me, I am telling the truth—even if you had twenty lives
To spend.
He has lived a long time in this land,
And caused strife without end;
Against his deadly hand
There's no way to defend.

"Therefore, good Sir Gawain, please, leave the man alone
And ride away by another road, for God's sake and your own.

2120   Take yourself off to some other land, where Christ may give you speed!
And I shall hurry home again, and further, I promise you—
That I shall swear on oath 'By God and all his hallowed saints,'
'So help me God and the holy relics,' and other oaths enough—
That I shall loyally keep your secret, and never let drop a word
That you ever tried to run away from any man I know of."
"Thank you so much," Gawain replied, though he said it with irritation,
"I should, I suppose, wish you good luck for caring about my welfare
And you say you will loyally keep my secret, as I believe you would.
But, though you kept it ever so close, if I hurried past this place,

2130   Fleeing away from him out of fear, in the style that you suggested,
I would be called a craven knight and I could not be excused.
So I will go on to the Green Chapel, to whatever challenge I meet,
And talk there to that knight himself, and tell him whatever I think;
Whether it brings me weal or woe, it will only be what Fate
Decrees.
He may be a fearsome knave,
Who could club me to my knees,

But God shapes things to save

His servants, should He please."

2140   "By Mary!" swore the other man, "Since now you have spelled it out

That you are bringing your own destruction down upon your head,

And it pleases you to lose your life, I will say nothing against it.

Here, put your helmet on your head, and take your spear in hand,

And ride this rough path down the stream by the side of that rock yonder,

Till it brings you to the bottom of the broad and rugged valley.

Then look to the glade not far away, a little off to the left,

And you shall see, set in that dale, the very chapel you're after,

And on its grounds the burly brute who keeps it in his care.

Now farewell, for the sake of God, Gawain the noble knight!

2150   For all the gold there is in the earth I would not go with you,

Nor keep you company through this forest even one foot farther."

With that, in the middle of the wood, the fellow yanked his bridle,

Kicked his horse's flanks with his heels as hard as he could spur,

Galloped him off across the glade, and left the knight there, all

Alone.

"By God's own self," he said,

"I will not weep or moan.

God's will must be obeyed,

His wishes are my own."

2160   Then he struck spurs into Gringolet, and followed the watercourse:

He pushed his way on past the rock, at the edge of a small thicket,

And rode along the ragged bank to the bottom of the dale.

Then he looked around on every side, and it seemed a wilderness.

Nowhere could he see a sign of a place where he might shelter,

Only high banks rising steeply, on both halves of the dale,

And rough and knobby rocky knolls, with sharp and craggy outcrops.

It seemed to him that the lowering clouds were grazed by the jutting rocks.

Then he drew his horse to a halt and checked him for a while
As he sat there, turning this way and that, to see where the chapel was.
2170   He saw no such thing on any side, and that seemed strange to him,
Except that a little off to the left in the glade was a sort of mound,
Or a smooth and rounded barrow on a bankside above the brim
Of the channel of a watercourse that was flowing freely through.
The brook was bubbling in it, as if it had come to a boil.
The knight then urged his horse along, bringing it up to the knoll,
Alighted from it gracefully, and at a linden tree
Attached the reins of his noble steed to one of the rough branches.
Then he walked over to the mound and striding all around it,
He turned over in his mind what this strange thing might be.
2180   It had a hole on one end, and the same on either side,
And it was overgrown with grass in patches everywhere,
And all was hollow inside the mound—nothing there but an old cave,
Or a crevice in an old crag? But which it was he could not

> Be sure.
> "Ah, Lord!" sighed the noble knight,
> "Can the Green Chapel be here,
> Where the Devil, around midnight,
> Might say his morning prayers?"

"Now," Gawain said, "without a doubt, this is a wasteland here.
2190   This oratory is horrifying, overgrown with greenery—
A very fitting place for that man who wraps himself in green
To do his duty and devotions—in the Devil's fashion.
Now I feel in my five wits that in fact it is the Fiend
Who has imposed this tryst on me, and will destroy me here.
This is a chapel of mischance—may it be checkmated!—
It is the cursedest kind of church that ever I came into!"
With his helmet high up on his head and his lance held in his hand

He climbed his way to the top of the roof above the rugged structure.

Then, farther up on the high hill, he heard, behind a rock,

2200 Beyond the brook, above the bank, a wondrously loud noise.

What! It clattered against the cliff as if it would cleave it in two:

Like somebody at a grindstone who was sharpening a scythe.

What! It whirred and whetted, like water through a mill!

What! It made a rushing, and a ringing, harsh to hear.

Then, "By God!" Sir Gawain said, "that weapon is being prepared

To welcome me with due respect, as a knight should be,

It appears.

God's will be done. To moan

Will never help me here.

2210 Though my life may soon be gone,

A noise won't make me fear."

With that the knight cried boldly out, as loudly as he could,

"Who is the master in this place, who holds this tryst with me?

For right now, good Gawain is walking, all around this place.

If any man wants anything, let him appear at once,

It's now or never, if he intends to get this business done."

"Wait!" shouted someone on the bank, somewhere above his head,

"And you will quickly have it all, that I once promised you."

Still he went on with that rushing noise, more rapidly for a while,

2220 Turning back to finish his whetting before he would come down.

And then he picked his way past a crag and emerged out of a hole,

Whirling out of a nearby nook, armed with a dreadful weapon:

A Danish axe that was freshly forged to pay the return blow,

With a mighty blade curving back on itself until it touched the helve;

It had been honed on a whetstone, and was full four feet in breadth—

No less than that if measured by the brightly shining belt!

And the man came out arrayed in green, as he had been at first,

His face and cheeks, his flowing locks of hair, and his green beard,

Except that now he went on foot, swiftly over the ground,

2230   Setting the haft on the stony earth and stalking along beside it.

When he came to the stream, he wouldn't pause at the water's edge to wade,

But vaulted across on his axe handle, and hurriedly strode on,

Fiercely grim, on a broad and grassy patch of ground that was cloaked

        In snow.

     Gawain greeted the seigneur,

     Bowing, but not too low.

     The other said, "Sweet sir,

     So—one can trust your vow."

"Gawain," the Green Knight then went on, "May God protect you now!

2240   I bid you welcome, sir, indeed, you are welcome to my place,

And you have timed your travels well, to reach it when you ought;

And you understand the covenant that was agreed between us:

On this day just twelve months ago, you took what was your lot,

And I, at this New Year, should promptly pay you in return.

And here we are in this valley, which is verily ours alone,

Here are no knights to part us, we may reel around as we please.

Take your helmet off your head, and receive your payment now.

Do not resist me any more than I resisted you

When you whipped my head off with a single whack of your battle-axe."

2250   "No," said Sir Gawain, "by the God who granted me a soul,

I will begrudge you not a groat for any hurt I receive;

Only hold yourself to a single stroke, and I will stay stock still

And offer no objection at all, whatever you want to do—

        Not one."

     He bent his neck and bowed,

     Exposing the bare white skin,

> Acting as if uncowed,
>
> Unafraid for him to begin.

Then all in a rush the man in green prepared himself to strike:

2260   He grappled and lifted the grim tool to give Gawain the blow;

With all the force in his massive frame he bore it up aloft

And swung it down as mightily as if to demolish him.

If he had followed through on that stroke as relentlessly as he started,

He, that man who was always brave, would have died from the force of it.

But Gawain caught a glimpse of the axe from the corner of his eye

As it came gliding down on him to destroy him in a flash,

And he flinched a little with his shoulders, shrank from the sharp iron.

The other man instantly checked his swing, held back the shining blade,

And then how he reproached the prince with many disdainful words:

2270   "You are not Gawain," the Green Knight scoffed, "who is held to be so good,

Who never quailed on hill or dale before an enemy horde,

And now you flinch from me for fear before you are even harmed!

I never heard of such cowardice on the part of that knight before.

I neither winced nor shied away, friend, when you swung at me,

Nor came up with some caviling argument in your King Arthur's house.

My head flew off and fell to my feet, and yet I never fled;

But you, before you take any hurt, are terrified in your heart.

I deserve, without a doubt, to be called the better man,

>   Therefore."

2280   Said Gawain, "I flinched once,
>
>   But will do so no more,
>
>   Though if my head falls on the stones,
>
>   It cannot be restored.

"But hurry up, man, by your faith, and bring me to the point,

Deal me the destiny that is mine, and do it out of hand,

For I shall stand and take your stroke and startle at it no more,

Until your axe has hewn into me: you have my plighted oath."

"Have at you then!" the other shouted, heaving it up aloft,

And grimacing as furiously as if he were out of his mind.

2290   He swung at him ferociously, but did not touch the man,

For abruptly he held back his hand before he might do him harm.

Gawain awaited the blow as he ought, and not a limb of his flinched,

But he stayed as still as any stone, or rather, like a stump

That is anchored into the rocky ground, locked by a hundred roots.

Then once again the man in green harangued him playfully:

"So, now you have your courage again, it's time to strike the stroke.

May that high knighthood preserve you now, that Arthur dubbed you with,

And save your neck from this next stroke, if it is able to!"

Gawain's fury grew more and more, and fiercely he lashed out,

2300   "Why, thrash away, you fearsome fellow, you waste time flinging threats!

I suspect that in your heart of hearts you have terrified yourself."

"Indeed," replied the other knight, "you speak so defiantly,

I will no longer delay you from accomplishing your mission—

Right now."

He took his stance to strike,

Puckered both lip and brow.

Sir Gawain didn't like

His chance of rescue now.

The knight lifted his weapon lightly, and let it so deftly down,

2310   With the sharp blade of the cutting edge onto the bare neck,

That though he hammered with his full force, it harmed him only so much

As to nick his neck on the one side, severing the skin.

The sharp edge sank into the flesh and through the shining fat

So the bright blood shot over his shoulders and out onto the earth.

And when Gawain glimpsed his own blood there, gleaming on the snow,

He sprang forth more than a spear's length and planted his feet to fight:

He grasped his helmet hurriedly and clapped it onto his head;
With a shake of his shoulders then he jerked his shield down into place,
And drew his bright sword from his belt and challenged fierily.

2320 Never since he had been a newborn babe in his mother's arms
Had he ever felt himself in this world to be half so happy a man.
"You can put a stop to your bold strokes, sir, and give me no more of them.
I have received one blow in this place, without resisting it,
But if you offer me any more, I shall pay you back at once;
I will repay you to the full, rely on it—and be

                                                    Your foe.

                        Only one stroke must fall—
                        Thus did we make our vow,
                        Which we pledged in Arthur's hall—
2330   And therefore, man, stop now!"

The great lord turned away from him and rested on his axe—
He set the shaft on the river bank and leaned on the sharp blade
And took a good long look at the knight who had taken a fighting stance,
How that plucky hero stood up to him, so fearless and undaunted,
Fully armed and free of dread: it warmed his heart to watch.
Then he addressed him cheerfully in his resounding voice
And with a ringing resonance he spoke thus to the man:
"Bold knight, don't be so fierce and grim, here on this grassy ground.
Nobody has used you ill, or in an unmannerly fashion,
2340 Nor acted against the covenant that we shaped at the king's court.
I pledged you one stroke, which you've had; you may hold yourself well paid;
I release you from the rest of it, and any further claims.
If I had not been nimble, perhaps, I might have dealt you a buffet
More out of anger, one that might indeed have provoked your wrath.
The first stroke, though, I threatened you for fun, with only a feint,
Not slicing you open with a slash—in this I gave you justice

According to the agreement we crafted your first night in my castle,

When you faithfully fulfilled our pact and were a man of your word:

All of your winnings you gave to me, as an honest man should do.

2350 The other feint I gave you, sir, because on the following morning

You kissed my wife and gave me back the kisses you had taken.

For those two days you took from me those merely feigning blows,

At your nape.

If a true man keeps his word,

Then he meets no mishap.

You fell short on the third,

And thus received your tap.

"For that is my garment you are wearing, that self-same woven girdle.

My very own wife gave it to you; indeed, I know it well.

2360 And I know all about your kisses, and all the things you did;

And as for your wooing by my wife, it was I who brought it about.

I sent her to assay your worth, and to tell the truth, I think

You are one of the most faultless men who ever went on foot:

As a pearl beside a white pea is so much more to be prized,

So is Sir Gawain, for his good faith, beside all other knights.

You were lacking only a little, sir, and your fidelity failed

Not out of wiliness or greed, nor was it for making love,

But only because you loved your life, so I blame you all the less."

The other, valiant as he was, stood silent a long while,

2370 So overcome with mortification he shuddered inside himself,

And all the blood in his breast flushed up and mingled in his face,

So that he winced and shied for shame at what the knight had said.

There at that moment the first words bursting out of him were these:

"A curse upon such cowardice and also covetousness!

In you are villainy and vice, that together destroy virtue."

The good knight then caught hold of the knot, unloosened the fastening,

And roughly flinging the whole belt to the lord who owned it, said,

"Look at it! There the false thing is, may the Fiend take it away!

Because I was anxious about your stroke, my cowardice could instruct me

2380   To accord myself with covetousness and forsake my character,

The largesse and the loyalty that truly belong to knighthood.

Now I am found to be faulty in them, and false, who have always feared

Treachery and untruthfulness—both of which lead to sorrow

And care!

I confess before you, Knight,

My faults in private here.

May your goodwill, if I might

Grasp it, keep me aware."

At that the other lord stood laughing, and answered amiably,

2390   "I hold it to be wholly healed, the injury that I had.

You have confessed yourself so cleanly, acknowledging your faults,

And you had your penance put to you at the sharp edge of my blade,

That I hold you cleansed of that offence, and purified as clean

As if you had never sinned at all since the day that you were born.

And I will give you this girdle, sir, with the gold along its hems;

For it is green as my tunic, Sir Gawain, and wearing it you may

Think back upon this little game, when you are pressing forward

Among other princes of excellence; this will be a noble token

Of the feat you performed at the Green Chapel, when you're among chivalrous knights.

2400   And now you shall, in this New Year, come back with me to my house,

And we shall revel away the rest of this glorious festival

Happily."

He pressed him hard, that lord:

"I think that with my lady

We shall bring you to accord—

She was your bitter enemy."

"Indeed I cannot," said the knight, and seizing hold of his helmet,

 He doffed it out of courtesy, and offered the lord his thanks,

 "I have lingered here quite long enough. Good luck to you and yours,

2410 And may He who determines all rewards repay you generously!

 Commend me to that courteous lady, your gracious, beautiful wife,

 Both to her and to that other one, my honored noble ladies,

 Who so adroitly have beguiled their knight with their devices.

 But it is not an unusual thing for a fool to act foolishly,

 Or for a man, through the wiles of women, to be brought down to grief.

 For in the same way Adam once was beguiled by one on earth,

 And Solomon by many women, and Samson was another—

 Delilah dealt him his destiny—and David afterwards

 Was blinded by Bathsheba and endured much misery.

2420 Now, since these were ruined by women's wiles, it would be an enormous gain

 To love them well, and not believe them—if any man could do that!

 For these were the favored ones of old whom fortune followed after,

 Yet they all went astray, although they were the most excellent men

          Under heaven!

    And all of them had the wool

    Pulled over their eyes by women;

    If I'm an equal fool,

    Might I not be forgiven?

"But as for your girdle," Gawain said, "May God reward you for it!

2430 I will wear *that* with all goodwill, though not for gain of gold,

 Nor for the cincture, nor the silk, nor for the long pendants,

 Nor for its costliness and prestige, nor the wonderful workmanship,

 But as a token of my transgression, so I shall see it often

 When I am riding out to renown, and remember with remorse

 The faultiness and the frailty that cling to the obstinate flesh,

 How it tends to be easily enticed to the spots and stains of sin.

And thus, when my prowess in battle shall prick me on to pride,

One look at this love-lace will remind me, and humble me in my heart.

But one thing I would like to know, so long as it won't offend you,

2440   Since you are the lord of yonder lands which I have been staying in,

So honorably received by you—may He repay you for it

Who holds the heavens above the earth and sits enthroned on high:

What are you called by your rightful name?—and then I will ask no more!"

"I will tell you that without deceit," the other man replied,

"Bertilak of Hautdesert is how I am known in this land—

Through the mighty force of Morgan le Fay, who is living in my castle,

And her skill in the magical lore and crafts that she once learned so well

Through the masterful arts of Merlin himself, many of which she acquired,

For she had pleasant love-dealings over a long while

2450   With that wise and excellent wizard—as is known to the knights from whence

You came.

Morgan le Fay, the goddess,

Therefore is her name.

Whatever his haughtiness,

There's no man she can't tame.

"She sent me out in this disguise to assail your handsome hall,

And put your vaunted pride to the test, to see if it held true,

The great renown of the Round Table, that is vaunted all over the world.

She sent me out as this marvel you see, to drive you out of your wits,

2460   And so distress Queen Guinevere that she would be startled to death

From horror at seeing that self-same knight, that ghastly phantom speaker

Talk from the head he held in his hand, facing the high table.

She is the one who lives at my home, she is that ancient lady.

Even more than that, she is your aunt, half sister to King Arthur,

She is the Duchess of Tintagel's daughter, whom noble Uther later

Fathered Arthur himself upon, who is now your sovereign king.

Therefore, my lord, I now beseech you, come and visit your aunt,

Make merry once again in my house, where my people love you so,

And I, my fellow, I, by my faith, bear you as much goodwill

2470   As any man living under God, for your great integrity."

Gawain said nothing to him but, "No!"—he could not, by any means.

The two knights then embraced and kissed, commended one another

To the high Prince of Paradise, and they separated there

                 In the cold.

         Gawain on his fair steed

         Made haste to the king's stronghold,

         And the knight in brightest green

         Rode to wherever he would.

Sir Gawain now went riding over many wild ways in the world

2480   On Gringolet, since through God's grace he had gotten away with his life.

Often he lodged inside a house, and often out of doors,

And met with many adventures in valleys and won many victories

Which I, at this time, do not intend to tell you all about.

The hurt that he'd received in his neck had healed and was whole again,

And he wore the gleaming belt about his body at all times,

Slantwise as a baldric that is fastened at the side,

The lace locked under his left arm, and tied there with a knot

As a token of the spot of sin—the fault he'd been guilty of.

And thus he came to the king's court, that knight, all safe and sound.

2490   Delight was wakened in that house when the noble folk found out

That Gawain had come back to them: they thought it a stroke of luck.

The king walked out and kissed the knight, and the queen kissed him as well,

And after them many a trusty knight who came to hail him there,

Asked him about his travels; he told his amazing story,

Describing all the tribulations he'd met with since he left—

How it chanced for him at the Green Chapel, the deportment of its knight,

The amorous actions of the lady, and at the last, the lace.

He bared the scar of the nick on his neck in order to show them all

What he had taken at that lord's hands for his unfaithfulness,

2500   His blame.

It tormented him to tell;

He groaned for grief, and pain—

The blood in his face upwelled

When he showed the cut, for shame.

"Look at this, lords!" the knight declared, handling the lace,

"This is the ribbon of the blame that I also bear on my neck,

This is the sign of the injury and damage I have deserved—

From cowardice and covetousness that both caught hold of me.

This is the token of the untruth that I was taken in,

2510   And I must keep on wearing it as long as my life may last,

For though a man might hide his offence, he cannot be rid of it,

For once it is attached to him, it never will come loose."

The king then tried to comfort the knight, as all the court did, also;

Laughing out loud at what he confessed, they amiably agreed—

The lords who belonged to the Round Table and all their ladies as well—

That each bold knight of that brotherhood should obtain a similar baldric,

A crossbelt slantwise from the shoulder, colored a bright green,

Which for the sake of that good man, they would follow suit and wear.

For that was agreed to be the glory of the renowned Round Table,

2520   And whoever wore it thus was honored, forever afterwards,

As is recorded, written down in the best book of romance.

Thus it came about in King Arthur's day that this adventure occurred,

And the books of British history bear witness to it as well,

Since Brutus, the bold, adventurous knight, first landed on these shores,

After the siege and the assault had been exhausted at Troy:

Finis.

Many exploits have been found
In times past, such as this:
Now He that once was crowned
2530   *With Thorns, bring us to bliss.*

AMEN

[HONI SOIT QUI MAL Y PENSE]

ENDNOTES

Notes on Previous Translations

These include: Neilson and Webster's prose of 1916; T.H. Banks's alliterative verse in the 1962 Norton Anthology, replaced there by Marie Boroff's more scholarly version in 1967, revised in 2013; the late James Winny's unpretentious, very useful line-for-line prose in the 1992 Broadview Press bilingual edition; W.S. Merwin's 2002 version in free verse. Two older paperbacks, the Penguin Classics by Brian Stone (1959, 1964, 1974) and the New American Library by Burton Raffel (1970) are fun to consult—Stone as the more solid scholar, Raffel as an outrageous provocateur. In 2006 two new translations came out. Penguin replaced the Stone version with a solid and scholarly work by Bernard O'Donahue. Faber and Faber has published an accentual alliterative version by Simon Armitage. William Vantuono and J.R.R. Tolkien added extensive scholarly apparatus to their respective verse translations. And there are others I have not read.

The expertise evident in several of these sources has often been helpful to me, a nonexpert on the Middle Ages. Especially I have benefited from the critical edition by Vantuono for summaries and interpretations of many details, and have made use of the meticulous glossary presented in the 1925 version edited jointly by J.R.R. Tolkien and E.V. Gordon. The most useful to me in making sense of the literal meanings have been James Winny's version and A.C. Cawley and J.J. Anderson's Everyman Edition of all four poems by the *Pearl* or *Gawain* Poet. The latter leaves the easy lines untranslated, moderate words are glossed in the margin, and only the more difficult passages are translated in prose footnotes. For the original text, I have relied on two standard current editions, Theodore Silverstein's critical edition (1974, 1984) and Malcolm Andrew and Ronald Waldron's *The Poems of the Pearl Manuscript* (2002).

John Ridland
Santa Barbara, California

JOHN RIDLAND WAS BORN IN London in 1933 to British parents. When he was two, his family immigrated to California where he has lived most of his life. Four years at Swarthmore College were followed by two in the United States Army in Puerto Rico. In 1956 he entered graduate studies at Berkeley where he met and married Muriel Thomas from New Zealand, a fellow graduate student. In 1964 he completed a PhD from Claremont Graduate University. Dr. Ridland taught English at the University of California, Santa Barbara, for forty-three years, including three years based in Melbourne as director for the UC  Education Abroad Program in Australia. His book publications include *A Brahms Card Ballad* (2007), first published in Hungarian translation (2004), *Happy in an Ordinary Thing* (2013), and a book-length translation of Petöfi's *John the Valiant* (1999). With his essential collaborator, Dr. Peter Czipott, Dr. Ridland has translated several other Hungarian poets, including Sándor Márai's *The Withering World* (Alma Classics, 2013) and Miklos Rádnoti's *All That Still Matters at All* (New American Press, 2014). In 2014 Askew Publications issued his epic poem, *A. Lincolniad.*

ALSO FROM ABLE MUSE PRESS

William Baer, *Times Square and Other Stories*

Melissa Balmain, *Walking in on People – Poems*

Ben Berman, *Strange Borderlands – Poems*

Ben Berman, *Figuring in the Figure – Poems*

Michael Cantor, *Life in the Second Circle – Poems*

Catherine Chandler, *Lines of Flight – Poems*

William Conelly, *Uncontested Grounds – Poems*

Maryann Corbett, *Credo for the Checkout Line in Winter – Poems*

John Philip Drury, *Sea Level Rising – Poems*

D.R. Goodman, *Greed: A Confession – Poems*

Margaret Ann Griffiths, *Grasshopper – The Poetry of M A Griffiths*

Katie Hartsock, *Bed of Impatiens – Poems*

Elise Hempel, *Second Rain – Poems*

Jan D. Hodge, *Taking Shape – carmina figurata*

Ellen Kaufman, *House Music – Poems*

Emily Leithauser, *The Borrowed World – Poems*

Carol Light, *Heaven from Steam – Poems*

April Lindner, *This Bed Our Bodies Shaped – Poems*

Martin McGovern, *Bad Fame – Poems*

Jeredith Merrin, *Cup – Poems*

Richard Newman, *All the Wasted Beauty of the World – Poems*

Alfred Nicol, *Animal Psalms – Poems*

Frank Osen, *Virtue, Big as Sin – Poems*

Alexander Pepple (Editor), *Able Muse Anthology*

Alexander Pepple (Editor), *Able Muse – a review of poetry, prose & art* (semiannual issues, Winter 2010 onward)

James Pollock, *Sailing to Babylon – Poems*

Aaron Poochigian, *The Cosmic Purr – Poems*

Stephen Scaer, *Pumpkin Chucking – Poems*

Hollis Seamon, *Corporeality – Stories*

Carrie Shipers, *Cause for Concern – Poems*

Matthew Buckley Smith, *Dirge for an Imaginary World – Poems*

Barbara Ellen Sorensen, *Compositions of the Dead Playing Flutes – Poems*

Wendy Videlock, *Slingshots and Love Plums – Poems*

Wendy Videlock, *The Dark Gnu and Other Poems*

Wendy Videlock, *Nevertheless – Poems*

Richard Wakefield, *A Vertical Mile – Poems*

Gail White, *Asperity Street – Poems*

Chelsea Woodard, *Vellum – Poems*

www.ablemusepress.com

CPSIA information can be obtained at www.ICGtesting.com
Printed in the USA
LVOW09*1914071016

507861LV00026B/211/P

9 781927 409763